THE WORD *IN OUR* HOME

A FAMILY PLAN FOR EXPLORING EVERY BOOK OF THE BIBLE

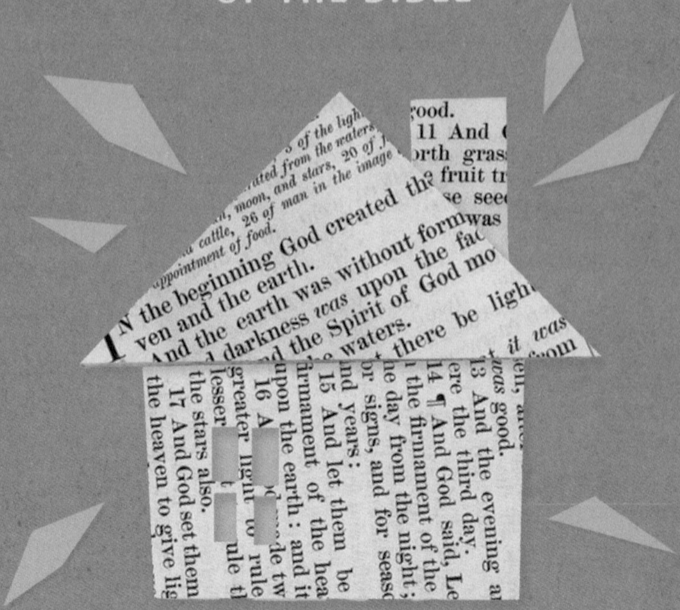

THE WORD IN OUR HOME

BARBARA REACH,
BEN REAOCH & STACY REAOCH

Moody Publishers
CHICAGO

Edited by Amanda Cleary Eastep
Cover design: Kaylee Lockenour Dunn
Interior Design: Brandi Davis

ISBN: 978-0-8024-3897-3

Originally delivered by fleets of horse-drawn wagons, the affordable paperbacks from D. L. Moody's publishing house resourced the church and served everyday people. Now, after more than 125 years of publishing and ministry, Moody Publishers' mission remains the same—even if our delivery systems have changed a bit. For more information on other books (and resources) created from a biblical perspective, go to www.moodypublishers.com or write to:

Moody Publishers
820 N. LaSalle Boulevard
Chicago, IL 60610

1 3 5 7 9 10 8 6 4 2

Printed in the United States of America

CONTENTS

INTRODUCTION FROM BENJAMIN REAOCH

As a son of the late Barbara Reaoch, author and former director of the children's division at Bible Study Fellowship, I had the privilege of growing up in a home where God's Word was central to everything we did. The Bible was not a dusty old book on the shelf. It was opened and read, memorized and applied, discussed and cherished. When my parents were serving as missionaries in South Africa, Mom started writing devotions for her grandchildren. Mom had discovered a way to disciple her kids and grandkids, even from afar. Those devotions were eventually published and have been a blessing to many other families as well.

This book is the culminating work my mom had dreamed of, and worked on, for years—a devotion taking families through the Bible from start to finish. Even as Mom battled cancer, this project remained a central focus of her efforts. As it became clear that her life on this earth was nearing its end, she and I spent some meaningful hours going through the many devotions she had written, and we discussed the overall vision of the project. Her passion to disciple the next generation was vibrant and inspiring, even to her final days. Her legacy continues in a multitude of memories, lives impacted, and resources written, including the book you now hold in your hands. We hope you and your family will be blessed as you engage with the life-giving, powerful Word of God!

WELCOMING THE WORD INTO YOUR HOME

Does God's calling to disciple your family feel more like a burden than a blessing? Do you feel ill-equipped and discouraged? You know you need to do something to help your kids love God and His Word, but you don't know how. Where can you turn?

The Word in Our Home is a tool designed especially for you! Using kid-friendly language, this resource is an interactive discipleship guide for families—one that helps adults communicate and apply powerful gospel truths. Parents have discovered that in just ten to fifteen minutes they can lead their family to read God's Word, talk about it, and pray together! With a target age of eight to fourteen, *The Word in Our Home* can easily be adapted to kids of every age.

This creative resource provides the dependable tool parents need to study the Word of God chapter by chapter with their family. Every chapter builds on the framework of Scripture: God's attributes, the gospel of Jesus Christ, and the essential truths of the Christian faith. Insightful discussion questions help parents cultivate God-centered conversations.

What to Expect

Each segment follows this format:

Read: The Bible is not like any other book. Reading God's Word together has eternal value. Each book of the Bible is divided into short readings of a few verses. Not every verse is covered, but the selected passages will help you follow the Bible's storyline from start to finish. If your children are older and have the ability and interest to read more, you can gently encourage them to do so (together as a family or on their own). An "icebreaker" question is included at the start of each book of the Bible to kickstart the discussion.

Listen: A brief lesson addresses the questions, "Who is God?" "What is His gospel plan?" and "What are the essential truths of the Christian faith?" It helps kids discover the answers to their hard questions from God's Word and leads them to see that truth is more fulfilling than competing arguments of a secular worldview.

Talk About It: Three questions are designed to take God's truth from a child's head to his heart. The questions probe the content of the Scripture passage, a spiritual principle, and personal application. These questions help children discover how truth intersects with their lives. Be prepared to get the conversation going. Pray to respond to your kids with understanding and not a judgmental tone. As your family responds honestly to God's Word and Spirit, they will begin to treasure the truth of Jesus.

Prayer: At the end of each book of the Bible, a short prayer is given as a springboard for your response to whatever God shows you about Himself, Jesus, and yourself. Prayer is a valuable way to let children know God is real and His presence is with us. Learning to pray for each other is a meaningful ending to this time of family worship.

Tips for Success

- **Be brief:** Better less than more.
- **Be real:** Ask God for the willingness to talk about how He is working in *your* heart.

- **Be consistent:** Aim to establish a regular time for *The Word in Our Home*. For some people it works best to read early in the morning before the family scatters. For others, reading a lesson at the close of the evening meal is an ideal time. Another popular time is late in the evening or just before bedtime. Every family must flex occasionally.

Get ready to enjoy the blessing of family discipleship! Prepare your own heart before you lead your family or others in *The Word in Our Home*. Ask your heavenly Father to guide you. Ask for insight about what questions to ask and how to promote discussion. Pray for God to give you a daily desire to make Jesus the focal point of your family.

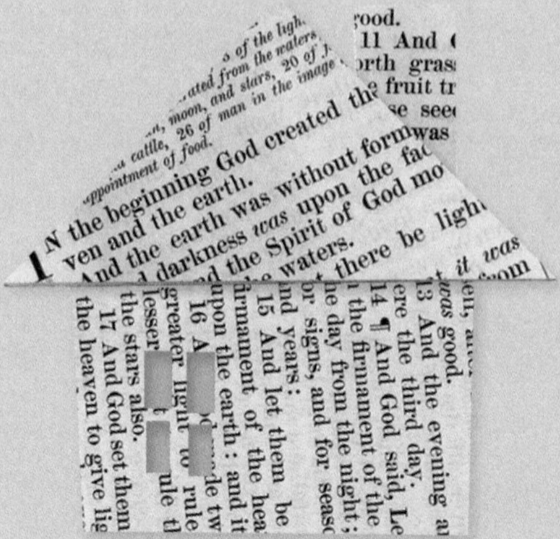

OLD TESTAMENT

GENESIS

Introduction

The book at the very beginning of the Bible tells us about the beginning of the universe. God created everything! God used His servant Moses to write the first five books of the Bible (Genesis through Deuteronomy). In Genesis we learn about the first human family: Adam and Eve and their children and grandchildren, all the way to Abraham, Isaac, and Jacob and their families, including the dramatic story of Joseph's life. God is the Creator of all things, and all people. And God leads His people and blesses them in order for them to be a blessing to others throughout the world.

> ICEBREAKER: What is your favorite part of creation that God made? Why?

Read Genesis 1:1–2

Who is God? God is the Creator of the universe and everything in it. God is perfect in love, goodness, wisdom, justice, and truth. Before there were blue skies, trees, and animals—and even before there were people—God was alive. People grow old and die, but God will never die. God will never change. A person needs help to build a house. They need a plan, bricks, and tools. But God is so powerful that He does not need instructions, materials, or tools to create. God built the whole universe without any help. There is no one like God.

TALK ABOUT IT

Who is God? What do we learn about God in these first verses of the Bible?

What did God create?

Why is it important to know God will never die or change?

Read Genesis 1:3–5

How did God create the universe? The Bible says that God made everything out of nothing by His powerful Word. God said, "Let there be light," and there was light. God's Word is just as powerful today. God's words are written for us in the Bible. God speaks to us in words that are not too hard for us to understand. Ask God to help you listen closely to His words to you. He will say to your heart, "Let there be light," so you can know Him and love Him (2 Cor. 4:6).

TALK ABOUT IT

How did God create everything?

How has God helped you understand His Word?

What will you ask God to do so you have a heart to know Him and love Him?

Note: When the Bible talks about our "hearts," it doesn't mean the physical organ in our body that pumps blood. It means the inner part of us that feels emotions and makes decisions.

Read Genesis 1:6–13

Did God create everything? God's powerful Word created the land, trees, sun, moon, stars, fish, birds, and animals. The world did not come to be by chance. The order and beauty in this world tell us there is a Creator, even to those who have never read the Bible (Rom. 1:20). God gave us the Bible to tell us why the world was made and how we can know the One who made the world. The Bible is not a science textbook, yet nothing in it contradicts science. The Bible is strong enough to stand up to our questions.

TALK ABOUT IT

Why did God give us the Bible?

When have you wondered if the Bible was true or could really help you?

What questions can you bring to God and ask Him to help you understand?

Read Genesis 1:20–25

What did God say is "good"? God said "It is good" when He saw the creatures He created to swim in the sea and fly high above the earth. When you hear a bird sing, you can praise God for His wisdom, power, and care in creating every creature. God made birds and sea creatures to be fruitful. That means God made them able to pass life on to baby birds and baby sea creatures. God is good, and He made many good creatures to live on the earth, and to multiply. These are special gifts for us to enjoy. God also gives us the good gift of His Son, Jesus. Those who trust in Jesus are given a new fruitful life (John 15:4–5; Luke 6:43–45). Like an apple tree grows delicious apples for us to enjoy, Jesus creates us anew so that we can show the goodness of God to others. When others see the spiritual "fruit" of our lives, it can help them to know our good and creative God.

TALK ABOUT IT

What does it mean for God's creatures to be fruitful?

What does it mean for those who trust in Jesus to be fruitful?

If you trust in Jesus, how do you see Him giving life to others through you?

Read Genesis 1:26–28

Why did God create people? God created people to know Him, love Him, and glorify Him. When the world was ready, God brought Adam and Eve into the beautiful garden He had made to be their home. This home was filled with luscious plants and friendly animals. The sun was their bright light in the day, and the moon gave soft light at night. In God's wisdom, He gave Adam and Eve a gift He did not give to any animal. God made them, and all people, in His image. God made us in a special way, to be in a relationship with Him and to represent Him. Animals are special, but people are much more special because God made us to be like Him.

TALK ABOUT IT

Why did God create you?

What does it mean to be created in God's image?

How would you describe your relationship with God—do you know Him and love Him?

Read Genesis 2:1–3

What did God do on the seventh day? God rested from His work of creation. After creating everything and seeing the goodness of all He had made (1:31), God rested. He was satisfied in the completion of this great work, like a talented artist is satisfied with a magnificent painting or sculpture. Everything in the universe, from the smallest blade of grass to the largest star, was perfectly created as God had planned. God gives our hearts rest from fear and doubt as we celebrate His work in creation . . . and His work through Jesus (Heb. 4:1–11). Apart from Jesus, we are restless, tired, unsatisfied, and without any hope of being complete. Our sin separates us from a holy God, and there's no amount of work we can do that will earn God's favor. But God sent

Jesus to finish the work of our salvation. Jesus' death and resurrection paid for our sin so we can celebrate new life with God. To trust in Jesus is to have a heart at "rest."

TALK ABOUT IT

How did God rest on the seventh day?

What work did Jesus finish so our hearts can rest?

How would you describe your heart—fearful or at rest?

Read Genesis 2:10–17

What did God tell Adam? God gave all kinds of gifts and blessings to Adam. He lived in a perfect world. He could play with all the animals and never get hurt. He could eat fruit from all kinds of trees. Best of all, Adam could talk with God in the garden. But God warned Adam not to eat of the tree of the knowledge of good and evil. He would die if he ate that fruit. God created us, and we belong to Him. God's people are to trust Him and do whatever He says.

TALK ABOUT IT

What did God tell Adam not to do?

Why are we to do what God says?

When has it been hard, but good, for you to do what God says?

Read Genesis 2:18–20

What job did God give Adam? Adam's job was to care for the earth. God and Adam had a loving relationship. Adam learned how to care for each animal and every unique plant. He enjoyed working in the garden with weed-free soil. When God brought the animals to Adam to name, Adam learned that only he, as a human being, was made in God's image. Adam loved God with all his heart. God created people to be in a loving relationship with Him. God created you for a loving relationship with Himself.

TALK ABOUT IT

What job did God give Adam?

Name some differences between animals and humans.

What are some jobs God has given to you?

Read Genesis 2:21–25

Why did God make Eve? God created Eve as Adam's special helper. From Adam's one body, God made Eve. God gave them the gift of marriage to join them together again as one. In marriage, God joins a man and woman's body, mind, and heart together as one. Adam and Eve loved each other, and they loved God. God wants us to have a relationship with Him, and He wants us to have a relationship with others. Marriage is one of the gifts He has given to a man and a woman to have a special relationship with one another.

TALK ABOUT IT

Why did God make Eve?

What is special about God's gift of marriage?

How do you show God you love Him?

Read Genesis 3:1–5

What did the serpent ask Eve? The serpent told Eve she could be "like God." This is different from what it means to be made in God's image. The serpent in the garden (who is really Satan), lied to Eve (John 8:44). Eve began to doubt God's love. She wondered if God was holding her back from something good. God's people, made in His image, learn to love and trust Him. The serpent wanted Eve to believe she could be "like God," knowing what only God can know.

TALK ABOUT IT

What did the serpent ask Eve?

How is "made in God's image" different from being "like God"?

How does Satan lie to people today?

Read Genesis 3:4–6

What did Adam and Eve do? Eve chose to believe the serpent's lies. Satan tempted her to do what is wrong. We will all be tempted to do what does not please God. Even Jesus was tempted by Satan. But Jesus did not listen to Satan's lies. Instead, He spoke the truth of God's Word and Satan left (Matt. 4:8–10). Eve could have stopped listening. She could have asked God for help. God always helps us when we call to Him. But Eve decided to eat the fruit. When she gave some to Adam, he ate it too.

TALK ABOUT IT

What did Adam and Eve do?

What did Jesus do when He was tempted?

When have you called to God for help with temptation?

Read Genesis 3:7

What happened when Adam and Eve listened to the serpent's lies? When Adam and Eve listened to the serpent's lies, they wanted to disobey. Adam and Eve were sinless and came into a world with no sin or evil. They were created with the desire to obey God. So when Adam and Eve ate the fruit, it was not just like someone saying something bad to God. In their hearts, they each pushed God away. It's like they said, "I don't trust You to decide what is best for my life. I don't want Your love. I want to live my way, not Yours." Adam and Eve chose to do what God told them not to do.

TALK ABOUT IT

What happened when Adam and Eve listened to Satan?

What was it like for Adam and Eve to disobey God?

When have you decided to do what you want instead of what God wants?

Read Genesis 3:8–15

What did God tell the serpent? God cursed the serpent, Satan, who had caused such great hurt. Satan had said God was lying about death. But Adam and Eve did die and now all human beings die. Then God made the best promise ever. God promised to send Jesus to rescue us from Satan's power (Heb. 2:14–15). Jesus would be born into the world as the "offspring" of a woman (Gen. 3:15). The hurt Satan caused Jesus would feel like a bruise on Jesus' heel. But Jesus would bruise the serpent's *head* when He rose from the dead. Our rescuer, Jesus, would free our hearts from the serpent's lies. All who trust in Jesus are rescued from Satan's lies and will live with God forever.

TALK ABOUT IT

What did God tell the serpent?

What was God's special promise?

How does God's promise take away our fear of death?

Read Genesis 3:16–20

What did God tell Adam and Eve? After Adam's sin, God's good gift of work became painful and hard. Now weeds have to be pulled before beautiful flowers can grow. After Adam and Eve's sin, God's good gift of children and marriage became painful and hard. Now anger has to be taken from our hearts before husbands and wives can love each other. All of us born into the human family struggle with the pain and hardship that began with Adam and Eve, our first parents. But God sent Jesus to take the pain of sin for us (Isa. 53:4–6). All who turn from sin and trust in Jesus are part of God's new family.

TALK ABOUT IT

Describe some ways that work has become difficult in our sinful world, how it's different than it was in the garden of Eden.

What did God tell Adam and Eve?

When have you felt the pain of your disobedience and selfishness?

Read Genesis 3:21–24

What happened to Adam and Eve? They had to leave God's special place because they disobeyed God's command. Sin had come into God's perfect world and now everything would die, even though it had been created to last forever. Since that time, people want to run away from God. Before God drove Adam and Eve out of the garden, He made clothes and covered them. And God would one day open the way back to Him (John 14:6). Jesus would open the way for us to come back to God.

TALK ABOUT IT

Why did Adam and Eve have to leave the garden?

What did God do for them before He made them leave the garden?

How can people come back to God?

Read Genesis 4:1–7

What happened to Adam and Eve? Eve had a baby and named him Cain. Then she had Abel. Cain became a farmer who grew crops for food. His offering to God was some of his crops. Abel raised sheep for wool. His offering to God was his firstborn and best sheep. Cain became angry that God accepted Abel's offering and not his (Heb. 11:4). But God loved Cain and told him to do what is right. God would gladly accept Cain, but Cain must say "no" to sin. God always wants what is best for us. But Cain wanted to do what he wanted instead.

TALK ABOUT IT

What was the difference between Cain and Abel?

Why was Cain angry?

When have you felt like a temptation to sin was crouching at your door?

Read Genesis 4:8–16

What happened to Cain and Abel? Cain was angry and jealous. He did not want to listen to God. He lied to his brother Abel and then killed him. God asked where Abel was but knew what Cain had done. God knows everything. Cain could have listened to God's warning. Instead, Cain received God's judgment for sin. Now Cain would have to look throughout the land to find food to eat. Cain thought his punishment was too hard. But Cain could have listened to God and obeyed Him (Ps. 19:9–11). God's Word, the Bible, warns us of the dangers of sin. It is wise to listen to God and obey Him.

TALK ABOUT IT

How did God warn Cain?

What happened when Cain did not listen to God's warning?

Have you listened to God's warning about the sin in your life and asked His forgiveness?

Read Genesis 6:9–22

What did God tell Noah to do? God gave Noah step-by-step instructions for building the ark. Through God's plan and strength, Noah built a huge ship with three floors. There was enough room for two of every kind of animal. People watching Noah must have thought he was crazy. Perhaps they tried to bully or distract him. Those who trust God and do what He says may be rejected by others, but God will never let them down. When it was time for God's judgment of the flood, God kept all His promises to Noah. God keeps His promises to all His children who trust in Jesus.

TALK ABOUT IT

How did Noah know how to build the ark?

What reaction can God's children expect from people in the world?

When have you been rejected because of your trust in Jesus?

Read Genesis 7:17–24

How did God care for Noah? God cared for Noah by protecting him from all mankind, which had become completely evil. God spared Noah from judgment. God warned Noah of the coming flood and told him how to build the ark. God called all the animals to come to Noah and then God closed the door to the ark. The flood came, but Noah, his family, and the animals were saved from God's punishment for the sins of evil people. God is good and promises not to let evil and violence go on forever. There will be another day of judgment (2 Peter 2:4–9). Our ark of safety is the Lord Jesus Christ. Every boy, girl, mom, and dad who has faith in Jesus will be saved (1 Peter 3:20).

TALK ABOUT IT

How did God care for Noah?

What does God promise to do about evil and violence?

What can you praise God for in this story?

Read Genesis 8:15, 20–22; 9:12–17

What was the first thing Noah did when he came out of the ark? The first thing Noah did was worship God. He built an altar and offered a sacrifice to God. Ever since sin entered the heart of man, God told us about the punishment for sin (Gen. 3:15). Sin against God is so awful that the punishment is death. But God is good and allowed an animal to take the punishment in the place of a person. The sacrifice of an animal could not take away sin, but it pointed to Jesus' death on the cross. One day Jesus would come to earth and be the sacrifice. Jesus died in our place so our sin can be forgiven (Heb. 10:11–14). God promised that He would not bring another flood like this one. And He gave a sign of this promise—the rainbow! When we see a rainbow in the sky, we can think of God's gracious promise.

TALK ABOUT IT

What was the first thing Noah did when he came out of the ark?

What does this teach us about God's relationship with His people?

What was God's sign of His covenant with Noah? What was God's promise?

Read Genesis 12:1

Why did Abram leave his home? Abram believed what God told him and left his home in Ur (Heb. 11:8–10). Abram knew God was greater than the gods his family worshiped in Ur. Still, leaving home would have been hard as Abram left everything he knew. Following God is not easy. Abram followed without knowing where he was going. But God promised to show Abram the way. We do not tell God where we will go and what we will do. God tells us to follow Him even when it means giving up what we love.

TALK ABOUT IT

What did Abram know about God?

Why is following God not always easy?

When have you followed God even though it was hard?

Read Genesis 12:2–3

What did God promise Abram? God promised that a nation of people would come from his family. And God said He would bless all the people on earth through Abram. How would God bless the people? God blessed everyone by sending the Messiah. The Messiah is the One God promised to save us from the punishment for sin—and He would come through Abram's family line. The Messiah is Jesus Christ.

TALK ABOUT IT

How would God bless the people through Abram's family?

Who is the Messiah?

Why did God send the Messiah?

Read Genesis 17:1–8, 15–16

When Abram was ninety-nine years old what did God tell him? God reminded Abram of His promise to give Abram many children, the land of Canaan, and the Messiah to come from his family line. God called His forever promises *covenants*. Abram and Sarai trusted God, even though they still had many questions. God gave them new names—Abraham and Sarah—as a reminder of what He promised to do for them. Trusting in Jesus means He gives us new hearts to know God and love Him.

TALK ABOUT IT

What are God's promises called?

What did the new names show Abram and Sarai about God?

What does it mean to trust in Jesus?

Read Genesis 17:9–14

What else did God give Abraham? God gave them a new sign of circumcision for them to know they belonged to God. By cutting off a piece of skin (foreskin), circumcision was a sign that the old life of sin was cut off and a new life of loving God had begun. The Bible tells us that when we trust in Jesus, God circumcises our heart (Rom. 2:29). God takes out our old heart that wants to sin and gives us a new heart that wants to love Him.

TALK ABOUT IT

What did the new sign of circumcision mean for Abraham?

What happens to our heart when we trust in Jesus?

If you trust in Jesus, how do you know you have a new heart?

Read Genesis 21:1–7

Why did God wait so long to keep His promise to Abraham and Sarah? God waited until it was impossible for their old bodies, as good as dead, to have a baby. God alone can bring life out of what is dead. Abraham and Sarah named their miracle baby Isaac, meaning "to laugh with joy." God promises another kind of new life—not in our bodies but in our hearts. Sin makes our hearts dead. It is impossible for us to make our dead hearts alive. Only God can give us this new life (John 3:6). Those who trust in Jesus receive new hearts, alive to God.

TALK ABOUT IT

What does the birth of Isaac tell you about God?

Why is it impossible for us to make our hearts alive?

What does "alive to God" mean to you?

Read Genesis 22:1–14

Why did God tell Abraham to sacrifice Isaac? God did this to give us a picture of the Father's love for His Son, Jesus, and to show us the meaning of a substitute sacrifice. Just as Isaac was Abraham's only son, Jesus is God's one and only Son. Isaac willingly offered himself as the lamb for sacrifice and Jesus willingly died on the cross as the sacrifice for our sin. God provided the ram as a substitute sacrifice so that Isaac didn't have to die. God provided His Son, Jesus, as a substitute sacrifice so that we don't have to die for our sins. God raised Jesus Christ to new life after He had been dead for three days. God's great love met our greatest need—forgiveness of sin—through the sacrifice of His one and only Son Jesus Christ.

TALK ABOUT IT

What did Abraham's test show us about God?

How was the sacrifice of Isaac a picture of Jesus' sacrifice?

Why or why not is the forgiveness of sin your greatest need?

Read Genesis 25:19–34

How did God bless Isaac? God passed on the promise of the Messiah to Isaac (Gen. 21:12). God gave Isaac and Rebekah twin boys—Jacob and Esau. Then God passed on the promise of the Messiah to Jacob. God does not choose people the way we do. We usually give prizes to people who do the best work. We choose people to be on our team who can help us win. But God does not choose us because of what we can do. God's grace gives us faith to believe in Jesus before we deserve it. God chooses us because of His grace (Rom. 9:10–15).

TALK ABOUT IT

What promise did God give Isaac and then his son Jacob?

How is God's way of choosing different from ours?

What does God's grace give us before we deserve it?

Read Genesis 32:22–32

What change did God want to make in Jacob? Jacob needed to trust God and let God lead his life. God made Jacob's body weak so that he could learn how to be strong in his trust in God. If God was going to use Jacob, He had to break Jacob's strong will (Hos. 12:2–5). After wrestling with God, Jacob walked with a limp. And God changed Jacob's name to Israel.

From then on, every step Jacob took reminded him of God's powerful love. And every time Jacob heard his new name, Israel, he remembered that God is trustworthy. God's will is so much better than our will.

TALK ABOUT IT

What change did God want to make in Jacob?

How did God cause Jacob to remember His powerful love?

When have you wanted God to do what you want instead of you doing what He wants?

Read Genesis 37:1–11

Why did Joseph's brothers hate him? They were jealous of Joseph. The brothers did not have beautiful coats like the one Jacob gave to Joseph. And the brothers did not have dreams like Joseph. They did not like the idea of Joseph ruling over them. But one day Joseph would rule over them and they would be grateful. Jealousy grew in the brothers' hearts. Jealousy is when we are angry that another person has something we want. The brothers wanted their father's love and attention. They also wanted to rule over themselves. Jealousy keeps us from seeing what God is doing.

TALK ABOUT IT

Why were Joseph's brothers jealous of him?

What is jealousy?

When have you been hurt by the anger and jealousy of others?

Read Genesis 37:18–36

What happened when Joseph looked for his brothers? Their jealousy made them want to hurt Joseph. Joseph's brothers decided to throw him in an empty well. Then Judah saw some men (Ishmaelites) coming on camels and said to his brothers that they should sell Joseph instead of killing him. Reuben began to fear what their father Jacob would do to them. The brothers lied to their father Jacob about what happened to Joseph. Jealousy makes us think of ways to lie instead of repent (turn away from sin) and tell the truth.

TALK ABOUT IT

What did the brothers' jealousy make them do?

When have you felt jealous of someone or angry at a brother, sister, or friend?

How did God protect Joseph's life?

Read Genesis 39:1–10

What happened to Joseph? The Ishmaelites took Joseph far away to Egypt. Potiphar, a captain in Pharaoh's army, bought Joseph as a servant. Joseph missed his home and family, but God had a plan and blessed him. Potiphar noticed Joseph's hard work and put him in charge of the whole house. Then Potiphar's wife wanted Joseph to sin against God. She lied to Potiphar and said Joseph was the one who wanted to do what is evil. Joseph did not do anything wrong, but Potiphar sent him to prison. Even through hard times, God has a plan.

TALK ABOUT IT

What happened to Joseph in Egypt?

What did Joseph know about God even through hard times in Egypt?

Think of some difficult situations in your own life that you can bring to God in prayer.

Read Genesis 41:25–32

How did Joseph get out of prison? After a long time waiting in prison, Pharaoh called him out. Pharaoh knew that Joseph could tell him the meaning of his dreams. Joseph told Pharaoh the meaning of the dreams came from God not him. Joseph knew the dream was God's way of telling Pharaoh what was about to happen. God is sovereign, which means God is in charge. God planned for seven years of sunshine and rain to make all the plants grow more than they usually do. More food would grow than the people could eat. There would be seven years of famine after that. Famine is when the plants do not grow and there is no food for the people to eat. God works all things in His time.

TALK ABOUT IT

Who told Joseph the meaning of Pharaoh's dream?

What does it mean that God is sovereign?

What did Joseph know about God that helped him wait so long in prison?

Read Genesis 41:33–44

Did Pharaoh like Joseph's plan? When Joseph talked about a plan to save food from the good years to use during the years of famine, Pharaoh knew it was a plan from God. Then Pharaoh made Joseph the leader of the people in Egypt to tell them what to do with the food. Pharaoh gave Joseph his special ring and a gold chain. Then Joseph was given another fine coat. Do you remember another time when Joseph was given a coat? The coat from Pharaoh was to show the people that Joseph was their leader. God is in charge over all His creation.

TALK ABOUT IT

What did Pharaoh know about the plan Joseph talked about?

What did Pharaoh give Joseph to show the people that Joseph was their leader?

What truth about God helps us not be discouraged when life is hard?

Read Genesis 42:1–5

Why did Joseph's brothers leave Canaan and go to Egypt? There was food in Egypt, and they were hungry because of the famine. They never thought they would see Joseph. Had they ever wondered what happened to Joseph? Or did they believe their own lie that they told their father, Jacob? Did they believe that Joseph was torn to pieces and left for dead? It is easy to start believing our own lies. But it is better to listen when God shows us the wrong we've done. God tells us what is right and wrong.

TALK ABOUT IT

How did God get Joseph's brothers to go to Egypt?

What is better than believing our own lies?

When have you felt hurt by someone telling a lie about you?

Read Genesis 42:6–17

Did Joseph let his brothers know who he was? No—before Joseph said who he was, he tested them to see if they were still jealous and cruel. Had they asked God's forgiveness? God used Joseph to convict his brothers of their sin. To be convicted is to feel the sting of what we've done wrong, to realize that we're guilty for disobeying God's commands. And to feel the conviction of our sin brings a desire to change. Conviction hurts but can lead us to repent (turn away from sin). It's like the painful feeling of steaming hot water on your hand, which makes you pull your hand away. God's Spirit makes us feel the pain of sin, so that we pull away from it.

TALK ABOUT IT

Tell the story of Joseph's interaction with his brothers in your own words.

How did God use Joseph to convict his brothers of their sin?

When have you felt the pain of conviction?

Read Genesis 46:28–34

What happened when Jacob and Joseph met? They hugged each other and cried for a long time. All the tears of sadness were mixed with tears of joy. God's plan for Jacob and Joseph included suffering. But through the suffering, God worked out His good plan. God planned that Jacob's family, who were shepherds, would live in Egypt where they would have food and land for their flocks. But living in Egypt meant Jacob's family might start to live like the Egyptians. And yet, God protected them. Egyptians did not like shepherds and gave Jacob's family land far away, in Goshen. In Egypt, Jacob's family would grow into a great nation. God takes care of His children.

TALK ABOUT IT

What good plan did God have for Jacob and Joseph through their suffering?

How did God plan to keep His children from starting to live like the Egyptians?

When has God used a hard situation to protect you?

Read Genesis 50:18–21

What did Joseph think about all that had happened to him? Joseph was hurt that his brothers hated him and threw him in the well. It had been lonely living in a prison so far from his father. But Joseph knew that nothing happens to God's children outside of God's loving and wise plan. God is sovereign. Joseph could see that God planned for him to be in Egypt to save many lives from the famine. God uses all things for the good of His children.

TALK ABOUT IT

What did Joseph know about God?

How do we usually think about the hard things in our life?

What things from your life has God used to make you more like Jesus?

Prayer

God, there is no one like You! You are all powerful and worthy of our praise. Thank You for Your beautiful creation and Your sovereign plans. Help us to be good stewards of all Your creation and help us to trust You even when life is hard.

EXODUS

Introduction

In the book of Exodus, we learn how God miraculously delivered His people from slavery in Egypt. Pharaoh was a very powerful ruler, but he didn't stand a chance against the power of almighty God. In the miraculous events of the Passover, the parting of the Red Sea, and the tabernacle, we see the truth of the gospel we believe today.

ICEBREAKER: Have you ever needed to cry out for help? What happened?

Read Exodus 1:8–11a; 2:23–25

Why were the people of Israel crying out for help? The Israelites had been slaves in Egypt for four hundred years. The new king in Egypt, Pharaoh, was afraid they would one day overpower him, so he made their lives difficult. The Israelites worked hard every day making bricks and doing whatever the Egyptians demanded. God heard their cry for help. God cared about them. He remembered His covenant that He made with Abraham, Isaac, and Jacob to make them a great nation and to give them the land of Canaan. God has a plan for our lives.

TALK ABOUT IT

What did the Israelites need to be rescued from?

What did God do when He heard their cry?

God sees us and knows our needs. When have you cried out to Him for help?

Read Exodus 3:1–12; 4:10–13

What is God calling Moses to do? God heard the cry of his people. He spoke to Moses from a burning bush, telling him of his plan to deliver the Israelites from the Egyptians. But God had a special plan for Moses. He was sending Moses to Pharoah, the king of Egypt, to deliver God's people from slavery. Moses is afraid. He doesn't think he has the right words to say or that he's qualified to do such a big job. God promises to be with him and to help Moses with what He calls him to do. God is faithful to equip us for whatever He asks us to do.

TALK ABOUT IT

How did God get Moses' attention?

What was His special plan for Moses?

Have you ever felt afraid to do something that you know God wants you to do?

Read Exodus 7:14–25; 10:21–29

What did God want the Egyptians to know? God wanted the Egyptians to know He is greater than all the gods they worshiped. The Egyptians believed that many gods ruled their life. They had a god for the water, the land, and the sky. God told Moses He would act with mighty judgment against these gods. God caused ten plagues to come upon Egypt. Each plague showed that God is greater than all other gods. God's judgment is always right. His judgment comes from His love. Worshiping other gods hurts people. God hates all evil because it hurts people. The plagues were God's warning to the Egyptians to repent and turn to Him.

TALK ABOUT IT

Why did Pharaoh have a hard heart toward God?

Why is it better to know the one true God than to worship other gods?

When we don't follow God, He may use a difficulty to call us back to Him. How might God warn people today to put Him first?

Read Exodus 12:1–14, 24–27; 13:8–9

Why did God give these instructions about the Passover? God gave these instructions to save His people from His judgment coming to the Egyptian people. It was a sad night for the Egyptian people who did not listen to God and obey His Word. There was loud crying in Egypt as the firstborn sons were killed in this plague. But when God saw the blood on the door frame, the firstborn son and animals were spared. In God's mercy, He allowed a lamb to take the punishment instead of the person who had sinned. At Passover, the blood of the lamb over the door meant the lamb was the substitute sacrifice for the sins of the people in that house. God made a way for sin to be punished and sinners to be saved.

TALK ABOUT IT

Why did God tell parents to talk about the Passover with their children?

How is the substitute sacrifice of a lamb a picture for us of what Christ did on the cross?

How is Jesus our Savior? Is Jesus your Savior?

Read Exodus 16:1–18

Why did God test the Israelite people with manna? God wanted the Israelite people to learn to follow His instructions. To follow God's instructions means to listen carefully to His Word and do everything He says. God planned to give the Israelite people bread from heaven. They were to follow God's instructions and gather the same amount of manna each day. Everyone had just what they needed whether they were big or small. God tested the people to teach them to follow His instructions. God tests us too. He wants us to learn to depend on Him to give us what we need. And God wants us to learn to follow His instructions. God wants us to learn how to be happy with whatever He gives us.

TALK ABOUT IT

How might God test your trust in Him?

When do you find it easy to complain?

How have you seen God provide for your needs today?

Read Exodus 20:1–11

What do the Ten Commandments tell us about God? The Ten Commandments tell us how to love God with all our heart. We are told to worship the one true God, never idols. The Israelite people worshiped idols of golden statues. But an idol can be anything we love so much that it takes the place of God in our hearts. We must ask ourselves what we love more than God. If we love wearing nicer clothes than anyone else, our idol might be ourselves. If we love to win the race and beat other people, our idol might be ourselves. We are all tempted to let ourselves become an idol, but God wants us to love Him more than we love ourselves.

TALK ABOUT IT

What does it mean to worship an idol instead of God?

When have you loved yourself more than you love God?

Has anyone kept all of these commandments?

Read Exodus 20:12–17

What do the Ten Commandments tell us about other people? The Ten Commandments tell us how to love other people as much as we love ourselves. God tells us to honor our mother and father. Many children disrespect their parents. But God wants us to listen to our mother and father and obey what they tell us. God said not to murder, break marriage vows, steal, lie, or be jealous of what belongs to someone else.

How do God's people obey His commands? Jesus obeyed in our place and was punished for sin in our place. When we trust in Jesus as our Savior, God forgives our sin and counts Jesus' obedience as belonging to us. God's Spirit changes our heart and gives us the power to obey His commands.

TALK ABOUT IT

Which commandments are you tempted to disobey?

What can you do when you're tempted to break one of God's commands?

How can you honor your father and mother?

Read Exodus 32:1–19

Why was making the golden calf a great sin? Making the golden calf was a great sin because it was an idol. After Moses was gone a long time, the Israelites made an idol that they thought would answer their prayers. An idol is anything we hope will give us what we don't think God can or will. An idol may be a video game, a friend, a sport or hobby, a goal—anything we want to love more than God. We can thank God that He wants to be the only God in our heart because He is the only One who gives us the true love we need.

TALK ABOUT IT

Why does God not want us to love idols?

What person, activity, or object has become more important to you than your love for God?

How will you learn to love God more than you love idols?

Read Exodus 40:1–2, 16–17, 32–38

What did God do after the people put the tent of meeting together? God showed Himself to the people in a cloud over the tent of meeting. In the Old Testament, God was with His people in a big cloud. When the people saw the cloud (or the fire at night) they knew God was right there with them. Why did God not just show Himself to the people? God has always shown Himself to us in creation, but because of our sin, we still do not see God face-to-face (Ex. 33:17–23). The Bible says God sent Jesus to earth so we could know Him (Heb. 1:1–3). And one day when we are in heaven and sin is completely gone, we will see God face-to-face.

TALK ABOUT IT

Why did God show Himself to the people in the cloud and not face-to-face?

How does God guide us today?

When have you read God's Word and known He was guiding you?

Prayer

God, we praise You that You hear us when we cry for help. You see us and know our needs. Help us to rely on You for the big things and the little things. Help us to love talking to You in prayer.

LEVITICUS

Introduction

This book was written shortly after the tabernacle was built. God tells His people how He wants them to live and how to worship Him. God is holy. We are sinful. It is amazing that God makes a way for His sinful people to be with Him.

ICEBREAKER: What is a rule that your parents have set for you? Why do you think they created that rule?

Read Leviticus 1:1–9; 2:1–3; 3:1–2; 5:14–16

Why is the book of Leviticus in the Bible? The book of Leviticus answers the question about how we can live with God. We cannot live with God without His forgiveness of our sins. The sacrifice of a lamb is a picture in the Old Testament of the greater sacrifice of the Lamb of God, Jesus Christ. The blood of Jesus Christ paid the penalty for sin. We need the cleansing of sin that comes through Jesus Christ.

In our current day, we do not have a tent of meeting or need for sacrifices, but we still need God's forgiveness. God is holy and we cannot come near Him without forgiveness of our sin. God had delivered the people of Israel from slavery in Egypt and given laws to them. If the people kept the laws, God would let them live with Him forever. But they broke the laws, and a lot of the people died because of their sin. God told them to build a tent of meeting and said He would come to live with them. How could God live with them? Would they all die? Leviticus is the answer to this question.

TALK ABOUT IT

What did God show the people about their sin?

How can sinful people come close to a holy God?

How are the animal sacrifices a preview, or pointer, to what would happen later when Jesus died on the cross?

Read Leviticus 16:1–22

What is atonement? It's a way sinful humans can be reconciled to a holy God. Reconciliation means something has to happen before a sinful, rebellious human being can approach a righteous holy God. God's holiness means He must remain separated from anything sinful or unholy. Therefore, it's impossible for us to enter His presence unless there is an atoning sacrifice. In the Old Testament, God instructed the Israelites to offer animal sacrifices. Later, Jesus came to be the final sacrifice for sin. For those who trust in Jesus, our sins are forgiven through His blood.

TALK ABOUT IT

Why did God ordain the Day of Atonement?

Why does our sin separate us from God?

How has God made a way for us to enter His presence?

Prayer

Thank You, Jesus, that You created a way for us to be forgiven of our sin. We praise You for the ultimate atoning sacrifice of Your blood. There is nothing we can do to earn Your forgiveness. It is a gift of Your grace. Help us to live in a way that is honoring to You.

NUMBERS

Introduction

The book of Numbers has many numbers in it. Chapters 1–4 and chapter 26 record the numbers from censuses that were taken of the Israelites. But it's a book of much more than numbers. In these chapters, we learn a lot about the Israelites' time in the wilderness, on their way from Egypt to the promised land. God is faithful to fulfill His promises, even though His people are often stubborn and fearful.

ICEBREAKER: Were you ever afraid and believed the worst would happen, only to be proven wrong? Tell us about it.

Read Numbers 13:1–3, 25–33; 14:26–31

Will the Israelites enter the promised land? The people were now close to the land God had promised them. But only two of the spies were full of faith, while ten of the spies were full of fear. And the fear was contagious. The people assumed the worst, rather than trusting God to keep His promises. Faith is simply obeying God in spite of how we feel, what we see, or what we think might happen. But unbelief and rebellion are often the result of being afraid of the obstacles before us. Because of the people's unbelief, God disciplined them by not allowing them to enter the promised land. Only the younger generation would be allowed to enter.

TALK ABOUT IT

What has God asked you to do? What has God promised to do for you? (See, for instance, Isa. 41:10 and Matt. 28:20.)

How were Caleb and Joshua different from the other spies?

When are you tempted to be afraid? What would it look like to trust God in those moments?

Read Numbers 21:4–9

How did God use snakes to teach the people about sin and faith? The Israelites continued to grumble and complain. They were impatient and ungrateful. God was angry with them and sent fiery snakes as a way of punishing them for their sin. How would you react if you saw a poisonous snake in your backyard? It would be scary! Many of the Israelites died from the snakebites. But God also provided a way for others to be healed. Moses held up a bronze serpent on a pole. Later, Jesus was lifted up on a cross (John 3:14–15). Whoever looks to Him in faith will be healed from the sting of sin and receive eternal life.

TALK ABOUT IT

Why were the people complaining?

How is the bronze serpent on the pole similar to Jesus on the cross?

What happens for those who look to Jesus in faith?

Prayer

Father, forgive us for times when we've been afraid and doubtful of Your promises. Strengthen our faith and help us to walk in joyful obedience. Guard our mouths from complaining and help us look to Jesus in faith.

DEUTERONOMY

Introduction

Deuteronomy is the last of the five books of Moses. Here we read the things Moses told the people just before they entered the promised land, and just before Moses died. The word *Deuteronomy* means "second law." You'll notice that the Ten Commandments that were in Exodus 20 are repeated here in Deuteronomy 5. You can think of this book like a father or grandfather giving godly advice to his family just before he goes to heaven. Moses reminds the people how gracious and faithful God has been to them, and that they should trust and obey the Lord.

> ICEBREAKER: What motivates you to obey a rule or command?

Read Deuteronomy 6:1–7

What happens in Deuteronomy? Moses preaches some final sermons to the people before he dies. In Deuteronomy, Moses reviews the law originally given at Sinai and applies it to Israel's life in the land of Canaan, which they're about to enter. Chapter 6 has a command that Jesus later talked about, the greatest commandment of all. Love is the best motivation for obedience. God's Word also motivates us with the warning of a punishment if we do not obey. But the best motivation for us to obey God is because we love Him, and we know His commandments are for our good.

TALK ABOUT IT

Why do you think Moses says, "Hear, O Israel"?

What are some ways you can love the Lord your God with all your heart, soul, and might?

Why is it important for parents to teach God's Word to their children?

Read Deuteronomy 31:1–8

What would happen after Moses died? Joshua would be the next leader of God's people. Remember Joshua? He and Caleb believed God's promises, even when others didn't. Now God is going to make Joshua the next leader, the one who will lead the people into the promised land. Moses tells Joshua to be strong and courageous. Moses tells Joshua not to be afraid. It takes courage to do the right thing when doing the right thing might be difficult.

TALK ABOUT IT

Why did Joshua need courage to lead God's people into the promised land?

What are some ways you need courage to do the right thing?

What is a promise in this passage that will help you obey God, even when it's hard?

Read Deuteronomy 34:1–12

How old was Moses when he died? Moses was 120 years old when he died. But he was still strong and had good eyesight! What did God show Moses right before his death? God took Moses up the mountain to look out over the promised land. Moses did not enter the promised land. But we know that Moses is with the Lord in heaven because Moses reappears in the New Testament with Jesus and Elijah on the Mount of Transfiguration (Matt. 17:3). Moses is an example of someone who believed what God said to him (Heb. 11:24–28). Knowing God is what made Moses great. And that's the thing that mattered most when Moses came to the end of his earthly life.

TALK ABOUT IT

Where did Moses die? Who buried him?

What makes Moses such an important character in the Bible?

Do you know God? Do you believe God's words to you?

Prayer

Father God, we know that You love us and that Your commands are good. Thank You for reminding us that our joy comes through obedience to Your Word. Help us to walk in line with Your Word, doing and saying what pleases You.

JOSHUA

Introduction

In this book, we shift from Moses to Joshua. Moses dies, and Joshua is the new leader. Now the Lord leads His people into the promised land! God keeps His promises to His undeserving people.

ICEBREAKER: Tell us about a time that you had to be strong and courageous.

Read Joshua 1:1–2

Who was Joshua? Joshua was Moses' assistant. Joshua means "God saves." He became the leader of the Israelites after Moses died. More importantly, Joshua was a servant of the Lord—he loved God and wanted to obey Him. Forty years before, Moses sent Joshua and eleven other men to explore the land of Canaan that God promised to them (Num. 13–14). The spies did not believe that God could give them the land. Only Joshua and Caleb believed God's promise. Joshua was a hero, but he knew the real hero was God. God has the power to keep His promises.

TALK ABOUT IT

Who was Joshua, and what does the name Joshua mean?

What did Joshua and Caleb believe about God?

Why is God the real hero?

Read Joshua 1:3–9

What did God promise Joshua? God promised to give Joshua all the land of Canaan just as He had promised Moses. God waited patiently, four hundred years, as the Canaanite people became more and more wicked. It may have seemed like the people got away with sin. Yet God waited and gave the people a chance to repent. God is merciful and warns all people of His certain judgment. Finally, the time came for God to punish their wickedness. Before Joshua went in to take the land, God told him to be strong and courageous. God promised to be with Joshua so he must not be afraid or discouraged.

TALK ABOUT IT

Why does God wait to judge sin?

What are some ways God warns people before judgment?

When has God helped you not be afraid or discouraged?

Read Joshua 1:10–18

What did Joshua tell the people? Joshua told the people all of God's promises. The Israelite people did not want to wander in the wilderness anymore. They were ready to go into the land God promised to give them. God told Joshua to tell the people to take the land, and He would fight for them. God promised to be with Joshua always. He would give him success and the land. God is trustworthy—He calls us to believe His promises and trust Him. God's children know He will give them strength to obey His Word.

TALK ABOUT IT

What did God tell Joshua?

How do God's children obey God's Word?

When has God given you strength to obey His Word?

Read Joshua 2:1–7

How did Rahab help the Israelite spies? Rahab took them up to the roof and hid them. She knew the king of Jericho wanted to kill them. Rahab heard about the Israelites' very powerful God. This God caused terrible things to happen to the Egyptians, until they finally let their slaves go free. This God parted the waters of the Red Sea to let His people go across the dry land. Then He brought the waters back together again, drowning the Egyptians when they tried to follow. Rahab knew nothing could stop the Israelites from taking the land God promised them.

TALK ABOUT IT

How did Rahab help the Israelite spies?

What did Rahab know about God?

What has God shown you about Himself?

Read Joshua 2:8–16

Why did Rahab help the spies? Rahab wanted to help them because she knew God had given the Israelites the land of Canaan. She knew the power of God and what He did for them. Rahab believed that the Israelites' God is the God who is everywhere—in heaven above and on the earth below. Rahab made them promise to help her and her family when they came into the land. God changed Rahab's heart, so she would trust Him. God made Rahab one of His children even though she was not an Israelite. It has always been God's plan to have people from all nations in His family.

TALK ABOUT IT

Why did Rahab help the spies?

Why did God plan for Rahab to be His child even though she was not an Israelite?

Who do you know who isn't a Christian? Pray that person turns to God and trusts in Jesus.

Read Joshua 2:17–24

What did the spies tell Rahab? The spies told Rahab to tie a red cord in the window. When the Israelites came into the land, they would see the red cord and know to spare Rahab and her whole family. God is merciful. He delights to save those who put their trust in Him. Rahab was not a good person. She had done many wrong things. But she believed in God's power not only to judge but to save. She trusted God's mercy and He saved her. God offers us the same gift. You can trust the mercy of Jesus Christ. He died on the cross to suffer the punishment we deserve. God saves all who turn to Him and trust in Jesus.

TALK ABOUT IT

Why did the spies tell Rahab to tie a red cord in the window?

Why was Rahab saved if she was not a good person?

Have you wondered if God will save you if you have done wrong things?

Read Joshua 3:5–7

How did Joshua get the Israelite people ready to go into the land? Joshua told the Israelites to get ready to see God do amazing things for them. They had to cross the Jordan River before they could enter the land. There was no bridge. The water was at flood stage—deep and flowing fast. Joshua told the priests to lead the way with the ark of the covenant. As soon as the feet of the priests touched the water's edge, the water stopped and piled up like a wall. As the people walked to the other side on dry ground, they knew God is almighty and always keeps His promises.

TALK ABOUT IT

What did the people need to do before they entered the land?

What did the people know about God?

How do you know God is almighty and always keeps His promises?

Read Joshua 3:7; 4:10–14

What did God do for Joshua? God gave Joshua the respect of the Israelite people. From the time Joshua led the people through the Jordan River, the Israelite people knew God was with Joshua just as He was with Moses. God told Joshua how to lead the people into the land. Everything happened just as God told Joshua. The people knew they could trust what Joshua told them about God. God is faithful to lead His people.

TALK ABOUT IT

What did God do for Joshua?

What did the people know about Joshua?

Who is God using to lead you closer to Him?

Read Joshua 4:4–11, 19–24

Why did Joshua tell the people to set up twelve stones? Joshua told the people to set up twelve stones to remember God is almighty and always keeps His promises. When parents saw the stones, they remembered to tell their children about God's power. When children heard how God made a way for the Israelites to get into the land, they knew God is trustworthy and faithful. We know God is trustworthy and faithful to us today. He has made a way for us to come to Him through Jesus. God promises that all who trust in Jesus will live with Him forever.

TALK ABOUT IT

Why did Joshua tell the people to set up twelve stones?

What did the parents tell their children about God?

How is God trustworthy and faithful to you today?

Read Joshua 6:2–5

What did the Lord say to Joshua? The Lord promised to give Joshua and the Israelites the Canaanite city of Jericho. God told Joshua, "I have given Jericho into your hand" (v. 2) as if it had already happened. God's plan for His people never fails. The Canaanite army was strong, and the Israelite army was weak. Jericho's walls were high and its gates were strong, but nothing is too hard for God. God's instructions seemed strange, but the Israelites needed to learn they could trust God's promises. God is faithful, and He gives His people the victory.

TALK ABOUT IT

What promise did the Lord give to Joshua and the Israelites?

Why did the promise seem impossible?

When has God told you to do what seemed impossible?

Read Joshua 6:6–21

What did the Lord do for the Israelites? God kept His promise and defeated the city of Jericho. Every day the soldiers marched around the city and seven priests blew trumpets. The Israelites knew God was with them because other priests carried the ark of the covenant. On the seventh day, they marched around Jericho seven times. The seventh time around, the priests blew a long blast on the trumpets. Joshua commanded, "Shout, for the Lord has given you the city" (v. 16). Just as God promised, the walls of Jericho collapsed. God is faithful, and His children can trust His promises.

TALK ABOUT IT

What did God do for the Israelites?

In what impossible situation do you need God's help?

When has God shown you that He is trustworthy?

Read Joshua 6:22–27

What did God do for Rahab? God saved Rahab and her whole family. Rahab was a Canaanite and had done many bad things. The Canaanites worshiped idols. God had given them hundreds of years to repent. All the Canaanites refused except Rahab. When she learned of Israel's God, she trusted Him. When the walls of Jericho collapsed, all the wicked Canaanites died. But God saved Rahab and her whole family. God is faithful to save those who put their faith in Him.

TALK ABOUT IT

In what way did God punish the people of Jericho for their sins?

Why was it so amazing that God saved Rahab?

What does Rahab's story teach us about faith, and about God?

Read Joshua 10:7–15

Who fought for the Israelites? God fought for the Israelites. Joshua prayed and God heard Joshua's prayer. The sun stopped for a full day. God's power created the sun. So it was not too hard for God to keep it in the sky longer until the Israelites won the battle. God acts in power as His children pray. God does not expect us to handle life's challenges on our own. Prayer is not only a key part of our fellowship with God but also a way God sovereignly accomplishes His will. Circumstances may or may not change but God never fails to do what is best for His children.

TALK ABOUT IT

What did God do in response to Joshua's prayer?

What do you learn from these verses about prayer?

How has God worked in your time of need, as you prayed?

Read Joshua 23:1–11

What did Joshua want the people of Israel to remember? Joshua wanted the people of Israel to remember the Lord God is their God. They were God's people because He loved them. They were not better than others, but God fought for them. For their sakes, He gave them the land He had promised. God also gave them His Word, and they were to be careful to obey Him. They were to hold tightly to the Lord. They were weak, but God gave each one the strength they needed to do His will. More than anything they were to be very careful to love God. What does it mean to be very careful to love God? To love God is to think deeply about His Word and ask for His help to live by what He tells us (Josh. 1:6–8).

TALK ABOUT IT

What did Joshua want the people to remember about God?

What does it mean to be very careful to love God?

How will you be very careful to love God?

Read Joshua 23:12–16

What warning did Joshua give the people of Israel? Joshua warned the people not to turn away from God. God wanted them to trust Him and not rely on the other nations. The people of Israel were not to marry anyone who worshiped other gods. God loved His people and knew this would be a trap. He did not want them to lose the good land He had given them. Joshua was about to die but the people knew with all their hearts that God had kept all of His promises. The people must take seriously God's warning to worship and love Him only.

TALK ABOUT IT

What warning did Joshua give the people?

What did God want for His people?

What warning is God giving you?

Read Joshua 24:14–23

What command did Joshua give the people of Israel? Joshua told the people to fear the Lord and serve Him only. For as far back as anyone could remember their families had worshiped other gods. They needed to decide whether they wanted to serve the one true God. Joshua said, "But as for me and my house, we will serve the LORD" (v. 15). The people said they would serve the Lord, but Joshua said they were not able to. How could such sinful people serve a holy God? Joshua told them to throw away their other gods and give their hearts to the Lord. Only God can make our sinful hearts able to love and worship Him.

TALK ABOUT IT

What command did Joshua give the people?

How can sinful people serve a holy God?

What does it look like in your life to choose the Lord and serve Him?

Prayer

Dear Lord, please help us to be strong and courageous. Help us to trust You and to follow where You lead. We don't want to be led astray to follow or serve other gods. You are the one true God, and we ask for Your help to remain devoted to You and to You alone.

JUDGES

Introduction

This book tells the sad story of God's people spiraling downward, again and again, as "everyone did what was right in his own eyes" (see the very last verse in the book). They are now in the promised land, but they don't yet have a king. The same cycle repeats itself. 1) The people disobey God. 2) God delivers them over to their enemies. 3) The people cry out for help. 4) God sends a deliverer (a judge). In this repeated cycle, we see the message of the gospel. 1) We have sinned. 2) We deserve God's punishment. 3) We must cry out to the Lord in repentance and faith. 4) God has sent His own Son, Jesus Christ, as our deliverer.

ICEBREAKER: What do you imagine angels to be like?

Read Judges 2:1–5

Who is the angel of the Lord? The angel of the Lord is Jesus before He became a man. He speaks God's Word because He is God. He reminded the Israelite people of how He had brought them out of slavery in Egypt and kept His special promise to Abraham to give the Israelite people the land. Now He came to ask them why they had disobeyed Him. He had warned them that other gods would become a trap to them. Now they would not have His help. The people were very sad and made sacrifices to the Lord. Sin is a trap, but God shows us our sin so we will turn to Him.

TALK ABOUT IT

Who is the angel of the Lord?

How did the angel of the Lord show God's grace to the Israelite people?

When has God shown you your sin, so you would turn to Him?

Read Judges 2:6–15

What happened after Joshua died? After Joshua died the people who outlived him kept on serving the Lord. But they did not tell their children all the great things God had done for Israel. When they died their children did not know God. The children grew up and turned from God to worship the false gods of the Canaanite people. God loved them too much to let them love other gods. As a parent disciplines a child, God caused their enemies to defeat His people. God disciplines His children, so they will turn to Him.

TALK ABOUT IT

Why did the children of the next generation not know God?

Why did God discipline His children?

Why does God discipline you?

Read Judges 2:16–23

How did God help the Israelite people? God helped the people of Israel by giving them judges. Judges were more like chiefs or generals than a judge in a courtroom. God was faithful to give them judges to save them from their enemies. But whenever the judge died, the people worshiped other gods again. They refused to give up their evil practices and stubborn ways. The Lord was angry. In God's goodness, He allowed the enemies of the Israelites to stay. They would learn to call to God for help. God is near to His children when they cry to Him for help.

TALK ABOUT IT

How did judges help the Israelite people?

What did the Israelite people learn about God?

When have you called out to God for help?

Read Judges 4:1–23

Why were the Israelite people in trouble? For twenty years, the Israelite people had worshiped other gods. God had sent the judge Ehud to save His children. But after Ehud died, the people went back to doing what is evil. The Lord sent Israel's enemies to turn their hearts back to Him. Sisera, the commander of Canaan's army, came with nine hundred iron chariots to oppress the Israelites. How did God help the Israelite people? God helped the Israelite people by giving them another judge, Deborah. Israel did not have chariots like Canaan's army, but Deborah gave the people God's promise. God would fight for His people. He used one woman alone in a tent to win the battle.

TALK ABOUT IT

Why were the Israelite people in trouble?

How did God help the Israelite people?

How does God save us from our enemy?

Read Judges 5:1–3

How did Deborah and Barak's song praise God? Deborah and Barak's song praised God for His love and power. They knew God won the battle for them. They praised God that the people of Israel willingly offered themselves to God. When the people turned back to God, they were willing to obey God even when it was hard. He gave them courage and skill for the battle. God's children still face many battles, but Jesus has already won our hardest battle with sin and death. As we willingly offer ourselves to Him, He fills us with His love and power.

TALK ABOUT IT

How did Deborah and Barak's song praise God?

How did the people of Israel offer themselves to God even when it was hard?

What are some worship songs you like to sing to God?

Read Judges 6:11–28

Why did the angel of the Lord come to Gideon? The angel of the Lord came to tell Gideon that the Lord was with him. Gideon was only a farmer, but the angel called him a mighty warrior. Gideon was the least important person in the least important family in the land. And yet God planned to use him to win the battle against the Midianites. Gideon was afraid, but he believed God's promise to be with him. He obeyed God's command and destroyed his father's altar to the false gods. God enables weak and fearful people to serve Him with their whole hearts.

TALK ABOUT IT

What did the angel of the Lord tell Gideon?

Why did God want Gideon to tear down the family altar to false gods?

Talk about some ways you can take a stand for the Lord.

Read Judges 6:36–40

Why did Gideon ask God for a sign? Gideon asked for a sign because he needed help to believe God would use him. He knew God was powerful to save, but he did not know God well enough to trust His will. Gideon asked God to make the fleece wet and then dry. God kindly strengthened Gideon to obey. God gives us His Word, His Spirit, prayer, and the wisdom of others to know His will. When we are afraid, God will give us strength to do what He asks. We can trust God's kindness to give us courage to obey Him.

TALK ABOUT IT

Why did Gideon ask God for a sign?

How does God help us know His will?

What makes you feel afraid to do God's will?

Read Judges 7:1–22

Why did God say Gideon had too many men? If the Israelites fought with many men, they would say, "We won the battle ourselves—we did not need God's help." God told Gideon to send home everyone who was afraid to fight. Only ten thousand soldiers stayed to fight the enemy. God does not want us to be foolish and think our strength saves us. God would save them by His strength and power, not theirs. God saves His children from their greatest enemy of sin, not by their strength, but through the death of His Son, Jesus Christ.

TALK ABOUT IT

Why did God tell Gideon he had too many men to fight the battle?

What lesson did God want them to learn through this?

How does God save His children from their enemy?

Read Judges 14:1–4; 15:16–20; 16:4–6, 21–22

Why was Samson so strong? God's Spirit made Samson strong to fight the Philistines. But Samson did not keep his promise to live for God. He knew he was not to love or marry a woman from the people who worshiped idols, yet he married a Philistine woman. Later Samson had a Philistine girlfriend, Delilah, who cut his hair. God's Spirit and strength left Samson. The Philistines blinded Samson and made him a slave. Samson failed to keep his promise to God, but God was still working to deliver His people. God completes His work even when His people go their own way.

TALK ABOUT IT

Why was Samson so strong?

How did Samson choose to live?

Discuss other examples (in the Bible, in history, or in your life) when God has used flawed and sinful people to accomplish His purposes.

Read Judges 16:23–31

How did God work on Samson's last day of life? On the last day of Samson's life, God once again gave him strength. The Philistines shaved his hair, blinded him, and made him a slave. But Samson's hair grew back. The Philistines took Samson to the temple of their false god to praise Dagon for giving them victory over Samson. In the crowded temple, Samson asked God for strength to deliver Israel. God's Spirit gave Samson such strength that when he pushed on the pillars the whole building collapsed, killing many Philistines. Samson knew he would die, but God gave him strength to complete His work. God's Spirit completes His work through His children.

TALK ABOUT IT

What did Samson ask God to do for him?

How did God give Samson strength to deliver Israel?

Samson was the opposite of Jesus in many ways. But how was Samson's death similar to Jesus' death?

Prayer

Father God, thank You for revealing Your plan to us through extraordinary ways. Forgive us for all the times we bow to other gods. Please convict us of our sin and help us to trust You, and Your ultimate deliverer, Jesus Christ.

RUTH

Introduction

This beautiful story happened during the time of the judges, and it bridges the gap from the time of the judges to the time of the kings. Here we learn about the great-grandparents of King David. They had a very unique love story! God is always at work, accomplishing His good plans even through very difficult times.

ICEBREAKER: Have you ever been rescued from trouble?

Read Ruth 1:1–18; 3:6–13

Who was Ruth? Ruth was married to Naomi's son. When Naomi's husband and sons died, she wanted to move closer to the rest of her family, who lived in Bethlehem. Ruth's family lived in Moab, but she really wanted to go to Bethlehem with Naomi. Ruth wanted to learn more about God, and Naomi knew God. Why did Ruth work in the barley field that belonged to Boaz? Ruth needed food, and God's law said that poor people could glean the grain from a field (Lev. 19:9–10). To glean means to pick up the grain that is left after a farmer harvests the crop. God took care of Ruth by leading her to the field of Boaz.

TALK ABOUT IT

Why did Ruth want to stay with Naomi?

How was God taking care of Ruth and Naomi?

Who is a person in your life who is teaching you about God?

Read Ruth 4:7–22

What is a redeemer? A redeemer is a person who rescues someone from trouble. Boaz was a redeemer to Ruth. After they married, Ruth had a baby (Jesse) who became the grandfather of David. This is the family line that leads to Jesus. Jesus is the greatest redeemer of all. He came to help us with our hardest problem in life—sin. In our hearts we are like Ruth, very poor and unable to help ourselves. But Jesus paid the penalty for our sin and made us part of His family.

TALK ABOUT IT

How was Boaz a redeemer to Ruth?

How is Jesus a redeemer to us?

What do you need to be redeemed from?

Prayer

Thank You, Lord, for Your amazing plan of redemption, which means to redeem, or save, us from our sin. Thank You for how You provide for us and protect us. Thank You for sending the ultimate redeemer in Jesus.

1 & 2 SAMUEL

Introduction

Samuel was an important leader whom God used to appoint the first kings of Israel. In these two books, we learn about King Saul and King David. As we see the faults and failings of these men, we realize we need a better King—King Jesus!

ICEBREAKER: What is something that you've had to wait for?

1 Samuel

Read 1 Samuel 1:9–11, 20, 24–28

God cared for Hannah. He also cared about His plan for the world. God works out His plan through His children's prayer. God is accessible to His children—so near that His Spirit lives in everyone who believes in Jesus Christ. Whenever you pray, God hears you. God does not always say yes, but He sees what you need and cares about you. Prayer is the way for us to connect with God. Prayer is also the way God chooses to work out His plan for the world. God works out His plan through our prayers.

TALK ABOUT IT

How did God care for Hannah?

How is God close to everyone who believes in Jesus Christ?

What happens when God's children pray?

Read 1 Samuel 3:1–12

Samuel had parents who loved God. He knew about God, but he had never spoken with God. Knowing about God is different from knowing God in a personal way. God is the most important person in the universe. He loves you and wants you to know Him personally. He invites us to know Him through faith in Jesus Christ. God gives new spiritual life to us, so we may believe the truth about Jesus. Jesus is our way to God. Through Jesus, we have a relationship with God. God makes it possible for us to have a relationship with Him.

TALK ABOUT IT

How would you describe Samuel's relationship with God?

How does God make a way for us to know Him personally?

How would you describe your relationship with God?

Read 1 Samuel 4:1–11

What was the ark of the covenant? It was the place God chose to live with His people. God is everywhere, all the time. But the ark showed the people our holy God's plan to live with His people on earth. God told the people how to handle the ark, but Eli's sons did not take God seriously. They thought they could come to God and do whatever they wanted with the ark. God is holy, and we cannot come to God any way we want. God invites us to come to Him today because of Jesus. Jesus is the way to God.

TALK ABOUT IT

What was the ark of the covenant?

What did Eli's sons think they could do with the ark?

How do we come to God today?

Read 1 Samuel 7:3–6

What did God's children learn about God? They learned God is holy and cannot be used to do what they want. They thought sin would make them happy. Instead, they were sad because of their sin against God. Samuel told them to repent—to turn from sin back to God. Samuel told them to get rid of their other gods. Our love of God grows as we turn from sin and love Him alone. Through faith in Jesus, we are filled with the Holy Spirit. He gives us power to say no to whatever dishonors God. Sin causes sadness, but God gives true happiness.

TALK ABOUT IT

What did God's children think would make them happy?

How do we become truly happy?

How do we get the power to repent and love God more than anyone or anything?

Read 1 Samuel 8:1–9

Why did the elders ask for a king? They did not want to wait for God's plan to send them His King, Jesus. All the nations around them had kings. They wanted to be like everyone else. The world changed them instead of them changing the world. God's children are tempted to turn away from God's plan to do what everyone else does. But Jesus Christ has rescued us from the power of sin. When we say yes to sin, the world changes us. When we say yes to God, He changes us, and He changes the world through us.

TALK ABOUT IT

Why did the elders ask for a king?

What surprises you about the Lord's response?

When have you been tempted to do what everyone else is doing?

Read 1 Samuel 10:17–24

The people of Israel wanted a king. They liked Saul because he was handsome and tall. But what they wanted would only harm them. God let them have what they wanted. God gave Saul everything he needed to be king. The people of Israel rejected God who is the loving all-powerful King. We can count on God always to be holy, to love us and to hate sin. God does not change. God's Word is like Him—it does not change. We can count on His promises, and we can trust Him always. The true King is God.

TALK ABOUT IT

What did the people want and why did they like Saul?

What did God think about the people of Israel's request for a king?

How is God lovingly calling you to turn to Him as your true King?

Read 1 Samuel 12:1, 16–25

God let the people of Israel have their way. But there were consequences. Samuel told them not to be afraid. If they and the king would turn to

God, it would go well for them. God forgives sin and offers new beginnings. Samuel warned things would go badly for those who kept on sinning and did not turn from evil to ask God's forgiveness. God may let us have our own way, but there will always be consequences. It is never too late to turn away from sin and trust in Jesus. God forgives sin.

TALK ABOUT IT

What warning did Samuel give the people?

What happens when we keep sinning and do not turn away from evil?

What does Samuel's warning mean to you? For what will you ask God's forgiveness?

Read 1 Samuel 15:13–16, 22–23

The reign of Saul, the first king of Israel, began well. But Saul began to put himself before God. Saul confessed sin but still blamed others. God loved Saul too much to let him keep disobeying. The consequences for his sin could not be undone. Saul's disobedience showed that he did not love God. Obedience to God is better than any good work we want to do for Him. When we obey God, our love for Him grows. We see that He gives us everything we need to obey Him. God is serious about obedience to His Word.

TALK ABOUT IT

What does Saul's disobedience to God tell us?

What does God think about our obedience to him?

How is God calling you to obey Him today?

Prayer

Father God, You are the loving, all-powerful God who rules over this world in truth and grace. I am sad that I still strive to get my own way instead of wanting Your way. Please help me want to obey You, and help my love for You to grow.

Read 1 Samuel 16:1–7, 10–13

God chose David to be the next king. People looked at David's size and age, but God looked at David's heart. God gave David love for God and for God's children. David learned a lot in his job as shepherd. He made sure the sheep had water and food. He watched the sheep day and night to keep them safe. David did not mind the hard work. He loved the sheep. The Bible calls God's children, sheep. God prepared David to take care of His children by taking care of sheep. God prepares His children to serve Him.

TALK ABOUT IT

What did God give to David?

How did God prepare David to take care of God's children?

How is God preparing you to serve him?

Read 1 Samuel 16:14–23

God brought David from taking care of sheep in the fields to the king's palace. It was not yet time for him to be king. David went to serve King Saul. Whatever David thought would be the best plan for his life, he let it go to serve where God guided him. God is our guide. He leads us where He wants us to go. David could play music. When David played his harp, Saul felt better. It was not easy for David in the king's palace. The Holy Spirit gave David power to serve Saul. God guides His children to places of service.

TALK ABOUT IT

How did God guide David?

How did God help David to serve where it was hard?

What hard place has God guided you to serve Him?

Read 1 Samuel 17:4–11, 32–37, 41–50

David was young and small, but God gave him the power he needed. David's battle with Goliath is not a make-believe story—it really happened. David learned that serving God can be scary. But God gave David the power he needed. All God's children battle giants—like struggles that make it difficult to serve God. But the battles teach us to trust God. Just as David won over the enemy Goliath, Jesus won over our greater enemy—sin and death. God gives His children His Spirit. God's Spirit gives us the power to live for Him and serve Him.

TALK ABOUT IT

What is amazing to you about God in this story of David and Goliath?

What do God's children learn about God in the battles of life?

How is God asking you to trust Him today?

Prayer

Father God, You are my guide. I don't always understand why serving You seems hard. Help me see how today's struggle is Your way of preparing me to serve You. Please help me trust You even though I can't see You. Teach me more about following You, my loving and powerful guide.

Read 1 Samuel 18:6–9, 12–16

Saul was angry and jealous. He was afraid David could take away his kingship. Instead of obeying God, Saul fought against God's plan to make David king. He did not ask God's forgiveness from his anger and jealousy. Anger and jealousy destroy those who fight against God. God helps His children be happy in big jobs or small ones. God's great power and kindness will help you do whatever job He gives. God gives His children power to serve with humility.

TALK ABOUT IT

Why did Saul fight against God's plan to make David king?

What does it mean to be jealous of someone who gets a big job?

When has God given a job you wanted to someone else?

Read 1 Samuel 19:1–6

God protected David in this time of suffering. The power of God's Holy Spirit rescued David from Saul. Like David, God's children suffer. Sickness, disappointment, and unkindness are part of living in a world full of sin. We cannot always understand why we suffer, but we can trust that God is good. No suffering comes to us that He does not allow for good reasons. God uses suffering to teach us how to depend on Him. We learn more about Jesus, who suffered for us. God's children can trust Him in suffering.

TALK ABOUT IT

How was David rescued from Saul?

Why is there suffering in the world and our lives?

What is something you can trust God with today?

Read 1 Samuel 20:12–17

The final goodbye between David and Jonathan shows the friendship of two men who trusted God. Jonathan, as Saul's son, was the next in line to be king. But he knew David was God's chosen king. Jonathan is a picture of Jesus, who would sacrifice what was rightfully His to do His Father's will. All God's children should expect opposition in this world from those who reject God. When you are rejected by friends and family because you belong to God, He is with you. God cared for David through Jonathan's friendship. God's children can expect opposition and God's care.

TALK ABOUT IT

What should all God's children expect in this world?

What does David and Jonathan's friendship show you about God's care?

What are some ways you can be a good and faithful friend to others?

Read 1 Samuel 24:1–20

David showed humility with Saul. Instead of punishing Saul himself, David depended on God. David's humble response caused Saul to feel bad about his sin. Are you, like David, learning to depend on God? God often teaches us by showing us our sin. You can depend on God for the strength to turn away from sin. Saul chose pride over peace with God. If you are in a hard place now, will you ask God for the humility to depend on Him? Then watch for God to show you His way through this difficult time. God guides those who depend on Him.

TALK ABOUT IT

How did David depend on God when he could have punished Saul himself?

What is the difference between humility and pride?

When you're tempted to seek revenge, how can you resist that temptation and depend on God instead?

Prayer

Father God, You are always at work in my life. Even through painful experiences, you are showing me more about my heart and about You. Thank You, Jesus, for being the perfect King. You told us that it would not always be easy to follow You. Please give me strength today as I depend on You.

Read 1 Samuel 25:2–3, 14–19, 23, 28–34

David loved God, but he was not a perfect person. God used Abigail to keep David safe and hold him back from doing what was wrong. If you are God's child by trusting in Jesus Christ, God will show you your sins. He may speak to you strongly through His Word, the Bible. He may bring another person to warn you or show you a way out of sin, just like He brought Abigail to David. God mercifully holds us back from doing what is wrong. God's warning of sin is God's mercy.

TALK ABOUT IT

What did Abigail do when David was ready to get back at Nabal for being evil?

Why does God bring other people to warn us about sin?

When has someone shown you a way out of a problem and kept you from committing a sin?

Read 1 Samuel 26:2–4, 7–11

Abishai saw a chance to kill David's enemy, Saul. David knew Saul was jealous and wanted to kill him. But David knew that to hurt Saul would be sin. David knew all sin is rebellion against God. David turned from sin and trusted God. This meant that David would wait for God to stop his enemy, Saul. Saul realized he was wrong to be jealous of David and want to kill him. But he did not obey God or ask God to forgive him. Only David turned away from sin and trusted God. All sin is against God.

TALK ABOUT IT

How did David think differently than Abishai?

What did David know about sin?

What does it mean for you that all sin is against God?

Read 1 Samuel 28:3–10

Saul trusted a medium (a person who claimed to speak to spirits) instead of asking God what to do. Saul panicked and looked for guidance that led him further from God. God warns us of going to the world or Satan rather than to the Lord and God's Word to know what to do. God calls His people to stay away from the evil spiritual world of demons, devils, spirits, horoscopes, palm-reading, superstitions, and fortune telling. God knows the future. He is faithful to guide us through His Word, prayer, and the wise advice of adults who follow the Lord. God calls us to trust His guidance.

TALK ABOUT IT

What did Saul do when he heard the Philistines were coming?

Why do we sometimes not wait for God's help?

Have you ever found yourself looking for a way out that is less than best?

Prayer

Father God, thank You for Your goodness. I admit that I do not always want to listen to the warnings You give me. When I am under pressure, instead of looking for a way out, help me remember to look for You. When I am tempted to lie or cheat just to get out of my problem, help me think about asking You for help instead of going my own way.

2 Samuel

Read 2 Samuel 2:1–7

Was it time for David to become king now that Saul was dead? David did not assume it was God's time yet. He waited for God to guide him. God led David to a city called Hebron. God was faithful to guide David throughout life. And God is faithful to His children today. God gives His children the Holy Spirit to live in them and guide them through life. As we read God's Word, the Holy Spirit helps us understand. God lets us ask Him about everything in our life. God expects His children to wait for His guidance.

TALK ABOUT IT

What did David ask God?

When might we assume it is the right time?

What guidance do you need from God today?

Read 2 Samuel 5:17–21

David struggled with the Philistines. But he learned to ask God what to do and wait for God's guidance. When we depend on our own good ideas instead of waiting for God, it is like trusting an idol. The Philistines learned that idols do not help win battles. God always knows what to do. God does not run late, get behind, or rush to get things done. God is always doing more than we can understand. It is always best to wait for God. We worship God when we depend on His help and wait for His guidance.

TALK ABOUT IT

What did the Philistines do with the idols they hoped would help them?

In what ways do we trust in idols? Think about how money, grades, success, popularity, the latest fashion or toys might become idols today.

With what struggle will you ask God for help and wait for His guidance?

Read 2 Samuel 6:1–15

David's greatest desire was to worship God. This meant the ark of God needed to be in Jerusalem. But God is holy. No one was to touch the ark. Uzzah's death was the consequence of sin against God. David learned that all people are not holy. How can we ever worship our holy God? In love, God gave His Son, who died on a cross in the place of sinners, to take our judgment for sin. All who by faith receive the truth of Jesus are forgiven. Through Jesus we, who are not holy, can worship our holy God.

TALK ABOUT IT

What happened as they were bringing the ark toward Jerusalem?

How did David react to this?

What are some ways you can worship God for His blessings to us?

Prayer

Father God, thank You for sending Jesus. I know that Jesus is the only way to You. Please give me faith to believe the truth of Jesus. Sometimes I trust my way of thinking instead of depending on You. Show me how I am trusting in the idol of myself. Teach me what it means to worship You alone.

Read 2 Samuel 7:1–9

David started out as a shepherd and God made him a king. David wanted to give back to God for giving him so much. God said no to David's plan to build a temple. David's son, Solomon, would build the temple. God had a greater plan for David—greater than he could have ever imagined! God promised to make David's name great, "like the name of the great ones of the earth" (v. 9). God brought David into His perfect plan for sending Jesus Christ. God's plans are so much greater than ours. God's plans are always best.

TALK ABOUT IT

What did David want to do for the Lord?

What was the Lord's response?

When has God's answer been "no" or "wait" to something you wanted to do?

Read 2 Samuel 7:10–17

God promised to build a living house from David's family to last forever. King David wanted to build a house for the Lord. But instead, the Lord promised to build a "house" for David. One day the greatest king, King Jesus, would come from the family line of David, to rule forever. The kingdom of the Son of God will last forever. All who trust in Jesus belong to His kingdom now and will live with Him forever. Through Jesus, God's promises are sure because of His power and faithfulness to His Word. His children will live with Him forever. God's promises are good forever.

TALK ABOUT IT

What kind of "house" did the Lord promise to build for David?

How long did the Lord say David's family and kingdom would last?

What questions do you have about God's forever kingdom?

Read 2 Samuel 7:18–29

David knew he deserved nothing, yet God had made him a king. How could God promise a forever throne to a human king? Only through Jesus Christ, the Son of God who would be born into the world from David's family. David prayed for God's plan, with courage. He knew that when God keeps His promises, people believe who He is. God always keeps His Word. Many years after David, God kept His promise: He sent His Son, the Lord Jesus, through the family line of David. God uses the prayers of His children to keep His promises.

TALK ABOUT IT

Why did David want God to keep His promise? (vv. 25–26)

What is God showing you about prayer?

How will you pray for God's plan for your life?

Prayer

Father God, thank You for your amazing plan to send Jesus. Please give me faith to know Jesus as the King of my life. Teach me to pray. Help me to want Your plan for my life. I want others to see You working in my life. Then they will know how great You are.

Read 2 Samuel 8:6, 14–15

David saved his kingdom from their enemies. When threats came against his people, King David fought for them. David depended on God to keep them safe. David's life is like the greater King, God's Son, the Lord Jesus Christ. Jesus defeated our strong enemy, Satan. Jesus won the victory over Satan for us. He died, and He came back to life! Jesus gives us help and victory over sin and Satan. Through Jesus, God's children have strength to stand for Him. God gives strength to His children.

TALK ABOUT IT

How did God use David for the good of the nation of Israel? (v. 15)

How would you describe the "enemies" we have today?

What kind of strength do you need from God?

Read 2 Samuel 9:3–10

Was Mephibosheth surprised by David's kindness? Mephibosheth was helpless to earn David's favor. David rescued him and promised life-long help. David and Mephibosheth's relationship remind us of the grace Jesus gives to us. Like Mephibosheth, we have nothing to give to our King. We have sin in our hearts. We are helpless to earn God's love and blessing. By God's grace, He sent Jesus to rescue us. Jesus took the punishment for sin that we deserve. God promises to forgive our sin and give us a new forever life. God, by His grace, rescues, forgives, and gives new life to His children.

TALK ABOUT IT

How did Mephibosheth respond to David's kindness?

How would you describe God's rescue plan for us?

How has God surprised you with kindness?

Read 2 Samuel 10:12, 17–19

God gave David and his people, Israel, power to win over their enemies. God defeated all David's enemies just as He promised. David's kingdom would be guarded from all their enemies in every direction, so God's people could live in peace. God gave David strength to faithfully obey Him for a long time. David loved God and knew his strength came from God's Word. For God's children, the Lord Jesus always wins over our enemy, Satan. We may have troubles in life, but nothing can defeat God's children. God's Word and His power give strength to His children.

TALK ABOUT IT

What did God do for David and His people Israel?

When has God's Word given you strength to win over sin?

What change will you make to have regular time with God in His Word?

Prayer

Father God, thank You that even though I do not deserve Your help, You sent Jesus to rescue me. Satan can easily defeat me. And my desire for sin is stronger than my willpower. But Jesus, You are stronger. Please help me change my priorities and make time regularly to read Your Word. I need Your strength to win over sin every day.

Read 2 Samuel 11:1–15

David's sin was not hidden from God. David did not use God's power to say no to temptation. God promises to show us a way out when temptation is too strong. God teaches us how to run from temptation—turn off the TV; don't take a second look when an image pops up on your screen; say no to friends who want to lie. God gives us His Word to change our hearts, so we love Him and hate sin. God's Spirit helps us understand if a choice will help or hurt us. God's children say no to temptation with His Spirit's power.

TALK ABOUT IT

How did David try to hide his sin?

What are some temptations that are hard for you?

Talk about a time when God helped you run from temptation.

Read 2 Samuel 12:1–10, 13–14

David's sin was great. He took Bathsheba and murdered her husband. Yet David's greatest sin was against God. Nathan's words made David think and stop making excuses. He felt sorry for his sin against God who loved him. David confessed his sin to God. David repented from his sin and God forgave him. David was forgiven but there are always consequences for sin. Sin always hurts us and others. We may be shocked at David's sin, but we must also admit our own sinful attitudes or actions. It is never too late to ask God's forgiveness. God forgives His repentant children.

TALK ABOUT IT

What did David think after he heard Nathan?

Why is it easy to see another person's sin and hard to see our own?

How does it help you to know God forgives the sin of those who repent?

Read 2 Samuel 12:24–25

Whether we are hurt by our own sin or the sin of others, God's kindness turns it all around for good. God changed Bathsheba's story from hurt to honor forever. Bathsheba was hurt because of sin. But she's included in Jesus' family line, which shows that God's plan is bigger than any of the wicked things people do. God promises to use even painful consequences of sin for your good and the good of others. God gives hope to His hurting children.

TALK ABOUT IT

What did God do for David and Bathsheba?

What is the most important truth about God you learned in this lesson?

How have you seen God use a difficult situation for good?

Prayer

Father God, You are powerful to help me say no to sin. I admit that many times I want to sin more than I want to obey You. Help me love You more than I love doing what I want to do. I need Your strength to win over sin every day.

Read 2 Samuel 13:6–16

Amnon disobeyed God and failed to respect Tamar. His violation, or harm, of Tamar shows he did not really love her. He was the cause of her intense suffering. Did Tamar's life matter to God? Yes! God, the Creator and judge of all, says every life is precious, and every crime against life is against Him. God's children who hope in Jesus have joy and are not held back by others' sins. God heals the wounds of sin in His perfect way. Sin is at the root of all our grief. Sin is selfish—it dishonors God and hurts people. All sin is harmful.

TALK ABOUT IT

How did Amnon's sin harm Tamar?

How would you describe sin?

How have you felt the harmful effect of sin?

Read 2 Samuel 15:1–4, 13–16, 30

David's son Absalom was next in line for the throne. Absalom worked out a plan to get the people of Israel to love him more than David. When David heard about Absalom's plan, he left Jerusalem. David knew that whatever happened, God would work to keep the city he chose for His people. David knew the destruction of sin. He was a sinner, and he was sinned against. Yet he also knew God's power to change the harmful results of sin. The Psalms tell us how God gave David joy even when very painful things happened to him. God's power can heal the harmful results of sin.

TALK ABOUT IT

What did Absolom do to win the favor of the people?

What did David do when he heard about Absalom's plan?

Have you ever felt the kind of disappointment David felt?

Read 2 Samuel 18:9–15, 31–33

Ahithophel, a counselor to King David, gave Absalom bad advice. He advised Absalom to treat David's wives as if they were his own. In this way, he would claim the kingdom as his own. Ahithophel also advised Absalom to murder his father, David. Joab believed murdering Absalom was for David's good. But David cried in intense grief for the harmful results of sin that Absalom experienced. David knew the harm of sin, yet he also knew God's power to change the harmful results of sin. Grace is God's power to change the harmful results of sin. God's grace is greater than sin.

TALK ABOUT IT

How did David react to the news of Absalom's death?

Why does the harmful result of sin cause us to feel hopeless?

How has God's grace changed harmful results of sin for you?

Prayer

I admit, God, that I sometimes feel hopeless because of the hurt from my sin and the sin of others. Please forgive me and help me to forgive those who have sinned against me. Give me Your joy, even if things stay hard. But please change the harmful results of sin in my life by Your powerful grace.

Read 2 Samuel 19:1–9

David seemed almost like a superhero. As a young boy, he had defeated Goliath. As the God-appointed king, he refused to kill his enemy Saul. But David was a sinner, not a superhero. David's sin hurt his family and split them apart. And David's sin had torn his nation apart. David wanted the men of Israel to get along with the men of Judah. But

David had added to the conflict between them. Was there any hope? God is able and willing to heal and make new what seems broken beyond repair. God can make new what sin has broken.

TALK ABOUT IT

What makes David a real person, not a superhero?

How does sin hurt a family?

What is God showing you about Himself?

Read 2 Samuel 22:1–7

David knew God's faithfulness and his own sinfulness. He knew God alone is righteous. God requires righteousness. But in ourselves, none of us is righteous. Before David saw it, he believed what God said about the day Jesus would come to live and die for our sin. In a similar way, without seeing it, we believe Jesus died on the cross as the payment for our sin. Faith is believing the truth about Jesus. David's life points to God's Son, Jesus, who came to earth from David's family line. God gives us forgiveness and righteousness through His Son Jesus Christ.

TALK ABOUT IT

What did David know about God and about himself?

How did David express what he was feeling in his heart?

What did David know about God that is also important to you?

Prayer

I admit, God, that I forget how my sin causes so much hurt to my family and friends. Please give me faith to turn from sin and turn to Jesus. I ask for Your forgiveness. Please make new what my sin has broken.

1 & 2 KINGS

Introduction

These two books continue from where 1 & 2 Samuel left off. David dies, and his son, Solomon, becomes the next king. But after Solomon, the kingdom splits in half. Most of the kings who come after are bad. They do not follow the Lord. But a few are good. We continue to see the people's need for a true, godly king who will lead them in righteousness. Sometimes by comparison (like with Solomon's wisdom), but mostly by contrast, these historical books make us look ahead to the one, true King—our Lord and Savior, Jesus Christ.

1 Kings

ICEBREAKER: If God told you that you could have whatever you asked for, what would you say?

Read 1 Kings 1:24–30

King David, when he got old, became very weak. Adonijah decided to make himself king in David's place. God gave David strength to do the right thing. That very day, King David made his son Solomon king. Adonijah tried to become king. But God had not forgotten David. Solomon would build God's temple and continue the family line to God's greater Son, Jesus. God is sovereign, and His promises to David would not fail. The Lord Jesus Christ would come from David's family line. God's promises are sure.

TALK ABOUT IT

What promise of God did David need to remember?

Why do we forget God's promises?

What promise from God do you need to remember today?

Read 1 Kings 3:5–15

God gave to Solomon a wise and discerning mind. Wouldn't you love it if someone said, "Ask what you want and I'll give it to you"? The question is, what do you and I really want? Solomon could have asked for health, wealth, or fame. But instead, Solomon asked God for wisdom. This request pleased God. God loves to give wisdom to those who ask.

TALK ABOUT IT

Why do you think Solomon, a man, called himself "a little child"? What was he saying about himself? (v. 7)

What did Solomon recognize about the task that had been assigned to him? (v. 8)

Why is it necessary to ask for God's wisdom in your life? In what areas of life do you need to seek God's wisdom—friendships, school, decisions about the future?

Read 1 Kings 8:12–21

When the Israelites were in the wilderness, God told them to build a tabernacle that represented His presence with them. Now that they are settled in the promised land, God instructs Solomon to build a more permanent structure. The tabernacle was a tent. The temple was built of stone and wood and gold. This is where the Israelites made sacrifices to the Lord. And it's where the ark of the covenant was placed, in the Most Holy Place, between the cherubim. The temple is like a little glimpse of heaven. God makes a way for sinful human beings to come into His holy presence.

TALK ABOUT IT

How was the temple different than the tabernacle?

Why did God have Solomon build the temple, instead of David? See 1 Kings 5:2–5.

How is the temple like heaven?

Prayer

Lord, Your plan is always best. I praise You for Your sovereign hand in my life. Turn my eyes to seek Your wisdom instead of my own. Let my desires be Your desires.

2 Kings

ICEBREAKER: Did you ever receive a gift or award that you felt like you didn't deserve?

Read 2 Kings 5:1–14

Naaman was a powerful man. He was in charge of Syria's army. But he had a serious skin disease called leprosy. An Israelite little girl was taken captive in a battle, and she had become a servant in Naaman's home. The little girl told Naaman's wife about Elisha, the prophet. Then Naaman's wife told Naaman. Then Naaman went to see Elisha, hoping to be healed. But Naaman didn't like what Elisha told him to do. Naaman wanted to be healed, but he wanted to be healed his own way. At first, Naaman was angry. But then his servants convinced him to do what Elisha said.

We are like Naaman. We have a heart disease called sin. We need Jesus to heal us, to forgive us. But it's not for us to choose how Jesus will do this. We certainly can't pay for it with money and gifts. We simply need to receive it as a gift. And it doesn't matter if you're a little girl or the commander of an army. Salvation comes in the same way to everyone—through humble repentance and faith in Jesus.

TALK ABOUT IT

What's surprising about this story?

Why was Naaman angry?

How is Naaman's healing like the salvation offered to us through Jesus?

Prayer

Lord, thank You that You don't give me what I deserve. Thank You that Jesus paid the penalty for me and freed me from sin. Help me to have a humble heart as I follow You.

1 & 2 CHRONICLES

Introduction

These books cover the same time period as 1 & 2 Kings. Both 2 Kings & 2 Chronicles conclude with the fall of Jerusalem and the people taken into exile. God disciplines His people for their rebellion. But God still has a plan!

1 Chronicles

ICEBREAKER: What purpose does God have for humans in the world?

Read 1 Chronicles 29:21–30

David knew he was alive for a purpose. He trusted God to keep his promises and was obedient to God's Word. God would bring Solomon and the kingdom the success He promised. David died and was buried in the City of David. God was with David—His chosen king and the man after His own heart. God's promises gave purpose to David's life. God's promises will give purpose to your life too. What God calls you to do will give glory to Him and great joy to you. God's promises give purpose to our life.

TALK ABOUT IT

What are your takeaway lessons from David's life?

What causes people to wonder if there is any purpose for their life?

How do your daily choices line up with God's purpose for your life?

Prayer

Father God, thank You for the life of Your servant David. He was not perfect, but he loved You and wanted Your purpose for his life. I admit that I have wondered what the purpose of my life really is. Help me to know that my life is not just an accident. You have made me for a purpose. Help me live for You and Your glory.

2 Chronicles

ICEBREAKER: Do you know of a child or teenager who has made a big impact in a positive way?

Read 2 Chronicles 34:1–7, 14–21, 29–33

Most of the kings in Israel and Judah were bad kings. They did not lead the people toward God, but away from God. Josiah was different. Josiah wanted to follow the Lord and lead the people to do the same. Josiah wanted the people to stop worshiping idols, so he tore down the altars to the false gods.

Judah had strayed so far from the Lord, they even lost the Book of the Law. But in Josiah's day, the Book of the Law was found again! Josiah was sad and scared. He knew that God must be angry at the people for all the ways they had disobeyed God's commands. Josiah led the people to repent of their sins and to follow the Lord.

TALK ABOUT IT

Was Josiah older or younger than you when he became king?

What did Josiah do to stop idol worship in Judah?

What does this passage of Scripture teach us about repentance and about the importance of reading God's Word?

Prayer

Father, thank You that You can use young and tender hearts to shine a light for You. Thank You for Josiah's desire to lead the people in following You. Thank You for the courage You gave him to confront sin and follow You. Even while I'm young, help me to be a shining light for You. Help me to be an example to others in following You instead of the world.

EZRA & NEHEMIAH

Introduction

The books of Ezra and Nehemiah go together. These books tell us about God bringing His people out of exile to return home. First, God enables the people to rebuild the temple. Later, they rebuild the walls around Jerusalem.

Ezra

ICEBREAKER: Have you ever seen a person change dramatically? How so?

Read Ezra 1:1–11

God's people had been so bad that God kicked them out of the promised land. But later, as He promised He would do, God graciously brought them back home. God is in control of everyone and everything. Even kings! Cyrus was the king of Syria, which was the place the Israelites were living since God sent them away from their homeland. God worked in the heart of King Cyrus, so that Cyrus wanted to help the Israelites return to their land and rebuild their temple.

TALK ABOUT IT

Where were the Israelites living? Who was Cyrus?

How did God provide for His people?

How has God provided for you?

Prayer

I'm thankful that You have power to change even the hardest hearts. I praise You for giving Your people favor in the eyes of King Cyrus. You are faithful to keep Your promises. Please help me to not turn away from You but to walk with You all my days.

Nehemiah

ICEBREAKER: Have you ever had to rebuild or remake something? What was the hardest part?

Read Nehemiah 8:1–8

The people were returning to Jerusalem. First, they rebuilt the temple. Then they rebuilt the wall around the city. Ezra and Nehemiah were both leaders of the people in different ways. On this particular day, the people gathered and listened to Ezra read God's Word to them all morning long! How did the people respond to this? They stood. They said, "Amen." They lifted up their hands. They bowed their heads and worshiped the Lord with their faces to the ground. There are many ways to show our respect for God's Word. Most of all, we should worship God for what He tells us in the Bible. Others helped Ezra read and teach the Scriptures. They read it and explained it, so the people could understand. This is a good example of what preachers and teachers of the Bible should do today. When we go to church, we should listen carefully to those who are teaching the Bible, so that we can understand more and more about God.

TALK ABOUT IT

How long did Ezra read from the Book of the Law?

List the things the people did as they listened to Ezra read the book.

What are some ways you respond to God's Word?

Prayer

Lord, I praise You that Your plan is the best plan. Thank You for Your faithfulness in keeping Your promises. Thank You for allowing the Israelites to rebuild the temple and for giving them an ear for Your Word. Help me to be faithful to listen to and obey Your commands.

ESTHER

Introduction

Many of God's people had returned home with Ezra and Nehemiah. But some Jews were still away from home, in Persia. Esther and Mordecai were among the Jews who were still away from home, under the rule of King Ahasuerus. Even though God isn't mentioned in this book, we can see His invisible hand protecting His people.

ICEBREAKER: What are your favorite kinds of parties? What activities do you do? What foods do you eat?

Read Esther 2:1–18

How did Esther become queen? King Ahasuerus had a party that lasted 180 days! He lavishly provided food and drink to his officials, servants, and even the people of Susa. On the seventh day, when King Ahasuerus had too much wine, he ordered his wife, Queen Vashti, to come before the king in order to show off her beauty to the other princes. The queen refused to be objectified and humiliated in such a way and would not come. King Ahasuerus was angry and embarrassed. Would other women defy their husbands following her example?

The king divorced her and sought a new queen. What the king did was evil, but God had a plan. Esther was one of the young women who was taken to the king's palace to prepare for meeting the king. Esther stood out among the women as she won favor in the eyes of everyone who saw her. Despite the poor choices of King Ahasuerus, God was at work in giving Esther favor in the king's eyes. Her beauty and contentment made her stand out among the women. The king made her his queen.

TALK ABOUT IT

Why did King Ahasuerus have to find a new queen?

What made Esther stand out among the women?

How might God be working in a difficult situation in your life?

Read Esther 2:19–3:11; 4:4–17

Why is Esther considered brave? Esther was raised in Susa by her cousin Mordecai (Est. 2:7). He worked at the king's gate and one day overheard some disturbing news. Two of the king's servants were planning to kill King Ahasuerus. Mordecai told Esther and she told the king on behalf of Mordecai. The king was saved! But another evil servant of the king was named Haman. Haman hated Mordecai because he refused to bow down to him. Haman planned to seek revenge. Haman wanted to destroy Mordecai's people, the Jews, and so spread lies about them to the king. The king agreed to destroy the Jewish people, not realizing that his very own queen was Jewish! Mordecai pleaded with Esther to intercede for their people. Yet Esther was afraid. Approaching the king without being called could result in death. Mordecai reminded Esther that God placed her as queen for such a time as this. No one else has the power to persuade the king. Esther decided to go, knowing "if I perish, I perish." Esther's willingness to sacrifice her life for the Jewish people points us to the sacrifice Jesus made for us.

TALK ABOUT IT

How did Mordecai save the king's life?

Why did Mordecai want Esther to talk to the king?

How might God be calling you to make a sacrifice in order to help others?

Read Esther 5:1–8; 7:1–8; 8:3–8

Why didn't Esther ask the king to save her people the first time? Esther was wise and discerning in when to ask for what she really wanted. She prayed and fasted about her approach to the king before she even met with him. In her first meeting, she merely invited the king and Haman to a feast. She gave the king wine and food, and spent time with him before she shared her concerns. It wasn't until the second feast that she poured out her heart to the king, telling him of Haman's evil plan to kill the Jewish people. The king was enraged at Haman's plan that would include killing his very own queen and had Haman hanged on the gallows (that ironically were built for Mordecai). Although the order to kill the Jews couldn't be revoked, the king allowed Esther to write a new law that would allow the Jewish people to defend themselves and spare their lives. Esther's wise words and humble approach to the throne had saved her people.

TALK ABOUT IT

What was the wise way Queen Esther made her request?

What happened to Haman and the Jewish people?

How might you act patiently and use your words with wisdom?

Prayer

Father God, I recognize that even when I can't see You, You are working in every situation in my life. Help me to trust that even when things don't go the way I desire, You are working for my good.

JOB

Introduction

We're not sure exactly when Job lived, but it was probably back during the time of Genesis, around the time of Abraham, Isaac, and Jacob. Job was a man who suffered much and eventually learned much from the Lord through his suffering.

ICEBREAKER: How do you respond when sad and difficult things happen in your life?

Read Job 1:1–22

Who was Job? Job was a man who loved God and obeyed God. The Lord allowed Satan to make Job's life very difficult. Satan thought that if Job's life became difficult, Job would stop loving and obeying God. What happened? Many hard things happened all at once. Did Job hate God because of it? No. Instead, Job worshiped. He was very sad. But he knew that God was in control, and that God is good.

TALK ABOUT IT

What surprises you about the conversation between God and Satan?

Why do you think God allowed Satan to test Job?

Are you able to worship God even when life is hard?

Read Job 2:1–10

Job is tested a second time. What's different? This time it is Job himself, who gets really sick. Job's wife did not help. She seemed to have lost hope in God and told Job to "curse God and die" (v. 9). But Job didn't do what his wife said he should do. Instead, Job continued to trust God. Job knew that God was still in control, even though his life had become miserable.

TALK ABOUT IT

What is the same in chapter 1 and chapter 2? What's different?

Why do you think Job's wife reacted the way she did?

What do we learn about God in these verses?

Read Job 38:1–4; 40:1–8

Much of the book of Job records a long discussion between Job and his friends. Job's friends were not always helpful. But God had lessons He wanted Job to learn. Finally, near the end of the book, God speaks. He speaks powerfully, out of the whirlwind. God asks Job questions that show Job who is in charge. Even if Job doesn't fully understand why these bad things have happened to him, he needs to be humble and trust God.

TALK ABOUT IT

What is the point of God's questions?

How did Job respond?

Why can it be difficult to trust God when bad things happen?

Read Job 42:1–17

What happens at the end of Job's story? Job humbled himself in repentance. Job had known a lot *about* God. But now God has spoken to Job powerfully and directly. Job now understands that he had been foolish to question God. Job's friends had some things they needed to learn too. God was angry with them, but God gave them grace. In the end, God blessed Job even more than before his hardships.

TALK ABOUT IT

What has Job learned about God?

What can we learn from Job about repentance and humility?

What's the difference between knowing *about* God and really knowing God?

Prayer

Dear Lord, You are all powerful and in control of all things. Thank You for Job's example of trusting You even in the midst of great loss. Help us to follow in his footsteps, trusting You with both the mountains and valleys in our lives.

PSALMS

Introduction

Psalms is the Bible's songbook. The psalms were written by a number of different people, in a variety of situations, expressing many different emotions. Whatever you're feeling, you can probably find a psalm that describes your joy, sadness, anger, thankfulness, despair, or praise. It's good to pray and sing and praise the Lord, whatever we're feeling.

ICEBREAKER: **When do you feel safest and most secure?**

Read Psalm 2

What does God tell us about His Son, Jesus? Jesus is called the Lord's Anointed (v. 2). To be anointed is to be set apart for God. David was anointed to be the King of Israel (1 Sam. 16:1, 13). And Jesus Christ was anointed, or set apart, by God to be the Messiah. Jesus is the King of the world. He is the King over all kings the world has ever known. He protects His people from those who want to hurt them. There is no King as strong and powerful as Jesus. Will the people on earth stop fighting God? God warns them to stop. They need to be wise and trust His plan. Nothing will stop God's plan, and one day Jesus will return to judge the people of the earth (Rev. 11:18). But "blessed are all who take refuge in him" (Ps. 2:12). There is happiness for people who stop fighting God and start trusting in Him. Jesus is our refuge or safe place.

TALK ABOUT IT

Who is God's Anointed One? What does that mean?

Why is it foolish for kings of the earth to disobey and rebel against God?

In what ways can you take refuge in Jesus? How can He be your safe place?

Read Psalm 53

Who does the Bible call a fool? It says that a person who does not believe in God is a fool. Why is it foolish not to believe in God? Because God gives us so many reasons to know that He is real. Every time we see the stars twinkle in the sky or taste cool water from a stream, we know that God is real. The stars and water did not happen by accident—they were made. It is foolish for someone to see the sun and stars, feel the cool fresh breeze on their face, and say there is no God. What does God say about this fool? God looks at the heart of every person and sees that no one wants to understand Him. All people have fallen away from loving Him. Not a single person is able to be good. Romans 3:23 says that "all have sinned and fall short of the glory of God." And God will judge those who do not believe in Him. But there is good news for those who want to believe in God. God saves those who trust in Him. They will belong to God forever.

TALK ABOUT IT

What does it mean to be a fool?

How many people want to understand God?

What does God see when He looks at our hearts?

Read Psalm 69:1–18

Why do we have trouble? Jesus tells us that in this world we will have trouble. We have troubles because Jesus had troubles. One day Jesus was troubled by the religious leaders who stole money from the people instead of leading them to worship God. At that time, Jesus' friends remembered Psalm 69:9, "Zeal for your house will consume me" (John 2:17). They learned that following Jesus means having trouble with people who do not love God. And when Jesus was talking to His friends before He died on the cross, He quoted Psalm 69:4. He told them, "They hated me without a cause" (John 15:25).

How does God help us? God says He wants us to tell Him about our problems. We don't have to try to deal with trouble by ourselves. Why do we need to tell God if He knows everything already? When we talk to God about our troubles, we can feel His love for us. When we listen to Him speak to us in His Word, we understand how to think rightly about our trouble. We learn that Jesus had troubles and knows how to help us.

TALK ABOUT IT

What troubles did the writer of Psalm 69 have?

How does God help us with our troubles?

What troubles do you have?

Read Psalm 91

Have you seen a mother bird hide a baby chick under her body? The feathers of her wings protect the baby chick from harm. This psalm says God protects His children too. Pinions are feathers. God doesn't have feathers, but when we are close to Him, we can trust him to protect us like a mother bird protects her young. What does God mean when He promises to show us His salvation (v. 16)? Salvation means to save someone from harm. One kind of salvation is to be saved from something that harms our body. But a greater salvation is to be saved from something that harms our spirits. Our spirit is the part of us that either believes God or doesn't. It harms our spirit not to love God. God wants our spirit to know and love Him. And He promises to save those who do. One day, our bodies will die, but God's salvation is the gift of living with Him forever.

TALK ABOUT IT

When has God protected you from harm?

How will you stay close to God?

What is God's salvation?

Read Psalm 95

What happened at Meribah and Massah? When Moses led the Israelites out of slavery in Egypt to the good land God promised, they walked through the desert. They got thirsty. And when there was no water, they got angry with Moses. They argued and complained. Moses called this place Meribah, which means quarreling, and Massah, meaning testing. Instead of believing God would help them, the people grumbled (Ex. 17:1–7). When they went through trouble, their hearts became hard. As noted in the discussion questions for Genesis 1:3–5, the heart is the place deep inside where we think, feel, and believe. A soft heart knows God is real and believes what He says is true. A hard heart does not believe God is real or that what He says is true.

How can we keep our hearts from becoming hard? The psalm tells us to worship God, to give Him the honor and thanks He deserves.

Even when we have trouble, we can praise God for being great and good. As God talks to you in His Word, don't harden your heart as the Israelites did. Listen and do what He says.

TALK ABOUT IT

What happened in Meribah and Massah?

Why did the Israelites have hard hearts?

How will you keep your heart from becoming hard?

Prayer

Lord, You are my refuge. Thank You for being my safe place when life feels like a storm. Help me to pour out my heart to You, to trust You in the midst of hard things. Help me to stay close to You.

PROVERBS

Introduction

We all need some good advice. The Proverbs are a collection of wise sayings, mostly from King Solomon whom God blessed with amazing wisdom. If you read all the way through, you'll gain counsel on: how to use our words, friendship, marriage and family, work and money, mercy and justice, and more.

ICEBREAKER: Who is the wisest person that you know? Why?

Read Proverbs 1:1–7

What is wisdom? Wisdom is different than being smart. A person can know lots of facts about things and still be foolish. In the book of Proverbs, God gives us many instructions that lead to wisdom. And it starts with fearing the Lord. When the Bible talks about the fear of the Lord, it's not the kind of the fear that makes us run away and hide. Instead, it's the kind of fear that makes us want to bow down and worship and obey. To fear the Lord is to respect Him and to be in awe of Him.

TALK ABOUT IT

Who wrote Proverbs?

How do you begin to grow in wisdom?

How can you learn to be wise?

Prayer

Father God, You are the source of all wisdom. Forgive me for fearing human beings instead of You. Help me to honor You by making wise choices all of my life.

ECCLESIASTES

Introduction

In this book, we hear King Solomon's thoughts about the meaning of life. The book might seem depressing. But there is wisdom we can find in these words.

ICEBREAKER: What do you think would make you happy in this life on earth?

Read Ecclesiastes 1:12–14; 12:9–14

What is the meaning of life? The meaning of life isn't gaining more things. If you think you will be happier once you have everything you want, you will be disappointed. Solomon, who had anything he wanted, tells of the emptiness of earthly pleasures. If you're looking for real meaning and purpose in this life, it won't be found "under the sun" (1:3). We have to look higher. Our purpose and meaning are found in fearing God and keeping His commandments. Life is short. Live for God.

TALK ABOUT IT

Why does Solomon sound sad?

What is the meaning of life?

How can your life be filled with meaning and purpose?

Prayer

Dear Lord, forgive me for trying to satisfy myself with things of this world. You are the true source of joy and peace. Help me to live my life with purpose and integrity, honoring You.

SONG OF SOLOMON

Introduction

This is another book containing the words of Solomon. Here we find Solomon's thoughts about love and romance.

ICEBREAKER: Have you ever been to a wedding? If so, what was your favorite part?

Read Song of Solomon 8:4–7

What is love? The Bible tells us God is love. A man and woman can be in love and get married. God created marriage as a special, loving relationship between a man and woman. A husband and wife are to enjoy God's gift of love. In this unique book of the Bible, we read about a husband and wife showing their love for each other. Marriage is also a way God teaches us about His love for us. Jesus loves His church the way a husband is to love his wife (see Eph. 5). The love between a man and a woman is very special. It can also be very powerful, which is why God's Word tells us that marriage is the promise a couple should make to each other, so they can enjoy their love the way God planned.

TALK ABOUT IT

How strong is love?

Can money buy love?

Why do you think God gave us a whole book of the Bible about the love between a husband and wife?

Prayer

Father, we thank You for Your beautiful design of marriage between a man and a woman. We praise You for how a marriage can be a picture of Christ and the church. Help us to honor Your beautiful plan for marriage.

ISAIAH

Introduction

God sent many prophets to speak His words to the people. Isaiah was a prophet to the southern kingdom of Judah. God showed Isaiah amazing things, including a vision of God's holiness (Isa. 6) and an incredible glimpse into the future about the suffering servant, who would be Jesus Christ (Isa. 53).

ICEBREAKER: If you could see into the future, what would you want to know?

Read Isaiah 6

What did Isaiah see in the temple? He saw the Lord Himself seated on a throne, in heaven (John 12:41). The angelic beings called the Lord "holy, holy, holy." God is more wonderful than anything the world has ever known. In contrast to God's holiness, Isaiah saw his own sin clearly. Isaiah had been looking at the sins of Judah, and then he saw his own sin. Sin is awful. It separates us from God. "To atone for" means to pay the penalty for sin. Payment for sin allows us to be reconciled or brought back to God. Isaiah was so grateful for God's mercy. He was ready to do whatever God said. Isaiah was told to keep telling people the truth about God. But the people had rejected God's message many times. Their hearts were calloused. A callous covers over soft skin with hard, thick skin. Like a callous, a person's soft heart can become hard toward God by ignoring His truth.

TALK ABOUT IT

How did Isaiah respond to the holiness of God?

What did the seraphim tell Isaiah?

What is the good news in this passage?

Read Isaiah 52:13–53:12

Who is the suffering servant? In these verses, Isaiah writes about Jesus, who is the servant of God who suffers in the place of God's people. Isaiah lived hundreds of years before Jesus came to earth. But God gave Isaiah glimpses into the future. God had Isaiah write down some of the amazing things the suffering servant, Jesus, would do to save us from our sins.

TALK ABOUT IT

What does this passage say about us? (See verse 6.)

Notice all the ways the passage describes how *He* suffers for *us*.

How does reading this passage increase your love for Jesus?

Prayer

Lord, I praise You for Your holiness. You are perfect and without sin. There is no fault in You. I see that I am so sinful, compared to Your holiness. Please take away my guilt. Thank You for sending Your Son as the suffering servant. Thank You that He suffered in my place.

JEREMIAH

Introduction

Jeremiah is known as the weeping prophet. There were often tears in his eyes as he brought God's messages to the people. And often the people didn't want to hear what Jeremiah had to tell them. Jeremiah was a prophet during the time when the southern kingdom of Judah was conquered by the Babylonian Empire.

ICEBREAKER: If you could ask God any question, what would it be?

Read Jeremiah 1

What did God tell Jeremiah? God told Jeremiah about His plan for Jeremiah's life. Even before Jeremiah was born, God planned for Jeremiah to be a prophet. A prophet is someone who tells people God's words and plans. God wanted Jeremiah to tell the people in Judah it was not right for them to worship other gods. The people in Judah needed a prophet to warn them about God's judgment. God always warns people before He judges them. But Jeremiah did not think he could do this. Jeremiah thought he was not old enough or strong enough to talk to people about God's judgment. What if they didn't like him or tried to hurt him because of what he told them? God loved Jeremiah and wanted him to have courage. God told Jeremiah He would give him strength and help.

TALK ABOUT IT

Why did Jeremiah think he could not do what God wanted?

What did God tell Jeremiah to give him courage?

What is God asking you to do that is hard?

Read Jeremiah 7:1–11

What did God tell Jeremiah to do? God told Jeremiah to go to the temple and tell the people to stop doing bad things. They were hurting each other and worshiping other gods. God is the only true God. He is the only One we are to love and obey. But some people worshiped the false god Baal. And after they worshiped Baal, they went to the temple and pretended to worship God. They thought if they did religious things at the temple God would keep them safe. Sometimes people think if they do religious things like go to church, say a quick prayer, or memorize Scripture that God is happy and will keep them safe. But God is not happy when we pretend to love Him. He wants us to love Him with our whole hearts.

TALK ABOUT IT

What did God tell Jeremiah to do?

What did God want the people to do?

What warning is God giving to you?

Read Jeremiah 12:1–17

Why does evil seem to go unpunished? Jeremiah wondered why God let people get away with sin. Why was God waiting so long to bring the justice He promised? But like someone watching a movie only halfway through, Jeremiah could not see the end of the story. In the end, God will judge sin and sinners. During our lives, God patiently warns people of His coming judgment. And His mercy gives people a chance to repent. God wanted Jeremiah to keep giving the people His message even though it was hard. God disciplines His people when they turn away from Him. But God also promises to restore them.

TALK ABOUT IT

What was Jeremiah's complaint?

What was God's answer?

Name some evils in our world that seem to be continuing on unpunished. How does this make you feel?

Read Jeremiah 18:1–12

Why did God send Jeremiah to a potter's house? God wanted to show Jeremiah that He is like a potter. A potter shapes things, like cups and dishes, out of clay. God is like a potter, and we are like the clay. God created you and shapes you to be what He wants you to be. God wants you to know that He has a purpose for you and things for you to do. We read His Word and listen to His Spirit to know what we are to do. We are most happy as we become what God made us to be.

Why did the potter have to reshape the clay? When we do not do what God wants, we need to be reshaped, like the clay. God loves us too much to let us go our own way. When we start to disobey God and act selfishly, He acts to get our attention. When God needs to change us, it may hurt at first, but we are most happy when we listen to God and start doing what He wants. This is what it means to repent of our sin.

TALK ABOUT IT

How is God like a potter?

Were the hearts of the people of Israel like soft or hard clay?

What is God doing in your life to shape you into the person He wants you to be?

Read Jeremiah 21:1–10; 38:1–6

Why did King Zedekiah's officials want God to perform a miracle? They wanted God to save them from their enemies, the Babylonians. Jeremiah told them God said they would be saved if they gave themselves over to the Babylonians. But if they tried to fight, they would all die. King Zedekiah and his officials could have listened to God and obeyed Him. But they did not want to. They hated Jeremiah for telling them the truth.

What did the officials do with Jeremiah? They lowered him into a deep well. The well did not have water and Jeremiah's body sank into the mud at the bottom. King Zedekiah and his officials thought they could stop God's truth by getting rid of Jeremiah. But the truth of God's Word can never be stopped. Jeremiah knew that trouble often comes to God's children because of their faithfulness to God. Many people did not like him. They called him names and wanted to hurt him. But Jeremiah also knew that God promises His children special strength for times of trouble (Phil. 4:13).

TALK ABOUT IT

What do you think were Jeremiah's greatest troubles?

How was Jeremiah faithful to God during times of trouble?

When has God given you strength in a difficult situation?

Read Jeremiah 31:27–34

What does God mean by a new covenant? A covenant is a promise. The new promise was different than the old promise. In the old covenant, God told the people to love Him with all their hearts (Deut. 6:4–9). But no one loves God all the time because we all have idols that we love more than God (Rom. 3:10–12). We love our stuff and ourselves more than God. No one ever loves God unless God changes their heart. God's work on our hearts is different than a heart surgeon who opens up blocked heart vessels. The surgeon unblocks the vessel so blood can flow to the heart. God works on our spiritual heart, changing our spiritual rebellion into a love for God and a desire to obey Him (Ezek. 36:26–27). When God changes the way we think and feel, we can love Him and believe His promises.

TALK ABOUT IT

Why do people need God to change their heart?

How is God's work in our hearts different from that of a heart surgeon?

Think about your own spiritual heart. How can you tell if God has given you a new heart?

Prayer

Lord, thank You that You long to hear our prayers. We praise You that You know our hearts yet love us anyway. Nothing is a surprise to You. Jeremiah persevered in telling people Your message. Help us to persevere in what You call us to do. Thank You for the gift of a new heart. We need You to change us from the inside out.

LAMENTATIONS

Introduction

Some people think that the prophet Jeremiah wrote the book of Lamentations, but we can't be sure. It was written around the same time Judah was conquered by the Babylonians.

ICEBREAKER: Are there things or situations in life that make you sad? What are they?

Read Lamentations 3:14–26

What is lament? Lament is an expression of sadness. *Lament*ations is a book of lament that expresses a person's sadness. The world is broken. We lament the pain and suffering and injustice in our broken world. There are consequences to sin. Because humans sin against God and against one another, there is a lot of hurt and sadness. We can tell God about all our feelings. We can bring our laments to Him. Even though we experience sadness in this life, we can wait on the Lord and trust that His love never ends. As Christians we can grieve and also hope in God at the same time.

TALK ABOUT IT

How is sadness described in these verses?

What are some things in the world and in your life that make you sad?

Talk to God about your sadness. What are some ways you can express your laments in prayer to God?

Prayer

Father God, our hearts ache with the injustice and sadness in this world. We cry out to You with our whole hearts and know that You see our tears. Please comfort us and be near to us when sadness overwhelms us. Help us to trust that You are good even in the midst of a broken world. Help us to remember our eternal hope in You.

EZEKIEL

Introduction

Ezekiel was another prophet around the same time as Jeremiah, to the southern kingdom of Judah. We can learn much about God through the writings of these prophets. God gave them special insights and visions to share with the people of their time that we can also learn from today.

ICEBREAKER: What is your favorite sweet food?

Read Ezekiel 1:28–2:7

What job did God give to Ezekiel? God gave Ezekiel the job of telling the people of Israel God's message. They were captives in Babylon because they did not obey God. They would not like Ezekiel for giving them God's message. But God was also going to give Ezekiel courage to give His words to the people. God gives us courage to do whatever job He gives us.

How did God give strength to Ezekiel? God gave Ezekiel His Spirit. When we trust in Jesus as our Savior, God fills our hearts with His Spirit called the Holy Spirit. Holy describes God: pure, perfect, just, and with no sin. The Holy Spirit gives us strength to do whatever God wants us to do (Zech. 4:6). If someone wears gloves to play in the snow, is it the gloves that build a snowman? No. It is their hands. We are like the gloves and the Holy Spirit is like the hand.

TALK ABOUT IT

What job did God give to Ezekiel?

How did God give strength and courage to Ezekiel for this job?

When have you been afraid to do a job God asked you to do?

Read Ezekiel 2:8–3:4

How did God give Ezekiel courage to do this job? God gave Ezekiel courage through His Word. God gave Ezekiel a scroll, which is like our Bible, God's Word. God's Word filled Ezekiel's stomach and tasted sweet. Like a big dinner gives strength to our body, the Bible fills our mind and heart with courage and strength. The Bible is sweet like honey because God's Word makes us happy knowing that God is good and has the power to do everything He tells us.

TALK ABOUT IT

What did God give Ezekiel to eat?

How is reading and studying God's Word like eating a meal?

In what ways has God's Word given you strength and courage?

Read Ezekiel 3:12, 23; 8:4; 9:3; 10:4

What is the glory of the Lord? The glory of the Lord is what God shows us about Himself. God wants us to know Him. When God shows us the blue sky and the dark night, we know He is powerful. When we learn He made our hearts to pump life-giving blood all around our body, we know He knows everything. When we see the sun rise and the moon appear each day, we know God is faithful. God shows us how creative He is when we see a butterfly or a tiny, colorful flower. We know He is powerful when we see a tall oak tree or lightening streak across the sky. God is kind to show us His glory so we will know Him and know that He is with us.

TALK ABOUT IT

How would you describe God's glory?

What have you seen of God's glory?

How does it encourage you to know that God wants us to know Him?

Read Ezekiel 10:18–19; 40:1–2; 43:1–9

What of His glory did God show Ezekiel? God showed Ezekiel special pictures of Himself and Ezekiel tried hard to put into words what he saw. Ezekiel knew God's presence with him was an awesome gift. And he knew it was an awful thing for God's presence to leave the people. God is holy, and as long as the people of Israel worshiped idols, God would not be with them. Would the glory of the Lord return? Yes. After God disciplined His people, He let them go back to Israel. They would worship God in the temple once again. But a day was coming when God would show us His glory more than He had shown Ezekiel or what we see in His creation. One day, God would send His Son Jesus Christ. All of God's glory is in Jesus (John 1:14). God sent Jesus, so we would know God. And those who trust Jesus as their Savior have God's Spirit living in them forever (1 Cor. 3:16).

TALK ABOUT IT

Why did the glory of God leave the people?

How does Jesus show God's glory?

How can you know God's Spirit is living in you?

Read Ezekiel 37:1–14

What did God show Ezekiel in the valley of dry bones? The dry bones Ezekiel saw came to life when God's Spirit breathed into them. The Bible tells us that we are all dead in our sins until God's Spirit gives us life (Eph. 2:4–5). The only time we have real life is when God's Spirit fills us (1 Cor. 2:12). When God puts His Spirit in us, we are born again. The moment we repent of our sins and trust Jesus as our Savior, we receive God's Spirit. God's Spirit helps us understand and love God as our Sovereign Lord. Then one day our body will be new too. When Jesus comes again, we will have a new body (1 Cor. 15:42–43). Only God, the Creator of the universe, can give us true life in Him.

TALK ABOUT IT

Why did God show Ezekiel bones without any life?

How did the dry bones come to life?

What does this passage show us about the power of God's Word?

Prayer

Thank You, Lord, that You equip us for whatever You call us to do. Thank You for equipping Ezekiel with Your Holy Spirit and giving him courage to speak Your words to the people. Help us to be strengthened by Your Word for whatever You call us to do. Help Your Word to be sweet like honey to us.

DANIEL

Introduction

Daniel is a well-known prophet because of the amazing stories of how God delivered him and his friends. Daniel was a prophet during the time when God's people were in exile in Babylon.

ICEBREAKER: When have you felt pressure to do something that you know is wrong?

Read Daniel 3:8–30

Daniel and his friends were taken away from the promised land to live in Babylon. They had to live among people who did not worship the one true God. God helped Daniel and his friends remain faithful even while living in a culture that opposed their faith. King Nebuchadnezzar wanted everyone to bow down to a tall gold statue. He wanted everyone to worship the statue he made. But Shadrach, Meshach, and Abednego wouldn't do it. They knew this would be wrong. So they were thrown into the burning, fiery furnace. God protected them in a miraculous way! Even Nebuchadnezzar took notice.

TALK ABOUT IT

What did King Nebuchadnezzar order everyone to do?

How did God protect Shadrach, Meshach, and Abednego?

In what ways does our culture pressure us to turn away from God?

Read Daniel 4:28–37

What happened to King Nebuchadnezzar? God humbled him. Nebuchadnezzar was a picture of pride. He thought that he was so great and powerful, and he wanted all the attention to be on him. God wanted to teach Nebuchadnezzar a lesson. And it's a lesson we need to learn as well. We can learn from Nebuchadnezzar's foolishness and pride. It's never good to be puffed up and to think that you are so great. Instead, we should give all the glory and credit to God.

TALK ABOUT IT

What is pride? What did Nebuchadnezzar say that was so prideful?

How did God humble him?

Where do you see pride in your own heart? Confess that to the Lord and ask Him to help you grow in humility.

Read Daniel 6:10–28

Now Darius was the king. And there were leaders who set a trap for Daniel. They were jealous because Darius made Daniel a top leader in the nation. The other leaders tricked Darius into making a new law: If a person prays to anyone other than Darius, they'll be thrown to the lions. Daniel knew this new rule had been signed into law. But Daniel still prayed to the true God, just like he had before. Darius tried to save Daniel, but the law was firm—even the king couldn't change the law he'd made. Daniel was thrown in the den of lions. But God protected Daniel.

TALK ABOUT IT

Notice some similarities between Daniel 3 and Daniel 6. In what ways did God protect His people, and also bring judgment upon their enemies?

How did God show His power? How did Darius respond?

In what ways is Daniel like Jesus?

Prayer

Lord, only You can make us walk in faith and not fear. Thank You for the courageous example of Shadrach, Meshach, and Abednego not bowing down to the gold statue. Thank You for giving them courage to be faithful to You even amid pressure. Help us, like You did Daniel, not to bow down to the idols of this world but to be faithful to Your Word.

HOSEA

Introduction

Hosea was a prophet to the northern kingdom of Israel. The message God gave to Hosea was not only a message of words, but a message Hosea lived out in his own marriage.

ICEBREAKER: Has someone ever broken a promise to you? How did you feel?

Read Hosea 1:2–11; 3:1–5

What did God tell Hosea to do? Hosea was a prophet with a unique ministry assignment. God told Hosea to marry a woman who would be unfaithful to him. Hosea's wife, Gomer, broke the marriage covenant. She ran away from Hosea and loved other men. This made Hosea's heart hurt. It's painful to show love and care toward someone who turns their back on you and runs into the arms of others. God wanted Hosea and Gomer's marriage to be a picture of how Israel had turned their back on God. God loved them and cared for them. But then God's people turned their backs on Him and bowed down to false gods (idols). Hosea had to pay money to get his wife back. Jesus paid with His life to bring His people back to Him.

TALK ABOUT IT

What did Gomer do that was wrong? What were the people of Israel doing that was wrong?

How do you think God feels when we ignore Him, run away from Him, and love other things more than we love Him?

How does the story of Hosea and Gomer give us a picture of God's love for His people and Christ's love for the church?

Prayer

Father God, You are so merciful and gracious. Thank You for Hosea's faithfulness to obey Your word and forgive Gomer again and again. Thank You for Jesus who paid the ultimate sacrifice for us so that we could be free from the penalty of sin. Please forgive us when we ignore You and break our promises to You. Help us to walk in joyful obedience.

JOEL

Introduction

Joel was a prophet to the southern kingdom of Judah. He lived earlier than Isaiah, Jeremiah, and Ezekiel. These books written by God's prophets are not all arranged in the order you would see them on a timeline. Joel's name means "Yahweh is God."

> **ICEBREAKER: Do you like insects? Which ones? Are you scared of insects? Which ones?**

Read Joel 1:1–4; 2:1–2, 12–13, 18–32

What do locusts have to do with God's judgment? God gave Joel a message about locusts, and about God's judgment. Remember the eighth plague (of the ten) that God sent upon Egypt (see Ex. 10)? In Joel's time, God sent locusts to judge His own people. Locusts are a kind of grasshopper. When many locusts come to one place, they can destroy the crops. They'll eat all the fruit and vegetables, so that there isn't enough food for the people to eat. One little grasshopper doesn't seem like a problem. But when there are swarms of them, they can be a real threat. Joel warned of "the day of the LORD" (2:1) which is a way of describing God's coming judgment upon sin. What is the right response to a warning about God's judgment? The right response is to repent of sin and trust in Jesus to forgive our sin. As Joel writes in 2:32, a verse quoted in Romans 10:13, "Everyone who calls on the name of the Lord will be saved."

TALK ABOUT IT

Do you like grasshoppers? What would you think of thousands of locusts taking over your favorite park?

What is "the day of the LORD" that Joel writes about?

How do you need to respond to the warning of God's judgment upon sin?

Prayer

Lord, we pray that You will pour out Your Spirit upon us. We want to be ready for Christ's return. We call upon Your name. Please save us from the punishment we deserve for our sins. Thank You for hearing our prayers.

AMOS

Introduction

Amos was a prophet to the northern kingdom of Israel, around the same time as Hosea.

ICEBREAKER: What would you enjoy about the jobs Amos had? See Amos 1:1 and 7:14.

Read Amos 5:6–24

Amos was a shepherd and a farmer. Amos preached God's words to Israel. In the time of Amos, many Israelites were wealthy. Times were good. They could build nice, big houses. They had plenty of good food and drink. But they were not helping the poor. In fact, they were hurting the poor in order to get more for themselves. They still pretended to worship God. But God knew their feasts, assemblies, offerings, and songs were just a show. God hates it when we take the good things He gives us and only think of ourselves. God hates it when we're mean to people who have less than we do, just because we want more and more. It's not wrong to have money, a nice house, or nice things. But God wants us to be kind and generous to others. God wants us to seek justice and righteousness.

TALK ABOUT IT

What were the people doing that was wrong?

Name some blessings God has provided in your life.

How can you promote justice and righteousness in your home, in your school, and in your community?

Prayer

God, we humble ourselves before You and confess our sins to You. We don't want our worship of You to be half-hearted or hypocritical. Convict us of ways we have mistreated others, especially anyone who has less than we do. We ask You that justice would roll down like waters, and righteousness like an ever-flowing stream.

OBADIAH

Introduction

Obadiah's name means "one who serves Yahweh." He wrote this sometime after the fall of Jerusalem. Obadiah's message is about the kingdom of Edom which was south of Judah.

ICEBREAKER: What would be some pros and cons of having a twin brother or sister?

Read Obadiah 1:1–21

What was Edom? Edom was the nation of people who were descendants of Esau. Remember Jacob and Esau from the book of Genesis? They were twins. Esau was born first, then Jacob. God's plan was to choose the descendants of Jacob (Israel) to be His special people. The descendants of Esau were the Edomites, and they lived on the other side of the Dead Sea. There was conflict between Jacob and Esau. And there was conflict between Israel and Edom. The short book of Obadiah is God's message of judgment upon Edom. The people of Edom were prideful, and they were enemies of God's people. So they would face God's judgment. What they had done to others would be done to them. God is judge over all the nations, and the day of the Lord will be for all the nations (v. 15). God judges sin. But God has also provided a way for prideful sinners to be forgiven, so they don't fall under His judgment.

TALK ABOUT IT

What have you learned about "the day of the Lord" from Joel, Amos, and Obadiah?

How does Obadiah describe the pride of Edom?

What did Jesus do to save us from God's judgment?

Prayer

God, please break down our pride and make us humble. We want to experience the happiness of humility. Help us to look to You, and to think less of ourselves. We want to enjoy You and the blessings that come with following Your Word.

JONAH

Introduction

Jonah is another well-known prophet (like Daniel) because of how amazing his story is! Jonah lived around the same time as Amos, but God sent Jonah to a different place. He took God's message to the people of Nineveh.

ICEBREAKER: What are your favorite parts of Jonah's story?

Read Jonah 1–2

Why did Jonah try to run away from God? God told Jonah, "Go to Nineveh" (1:2). Nineveh was the capital of Assyria, and they were Israel's enemies. Jonah didn't want to go. He couldn't imagine facing such bad people. So Jonah did something foolish. He boarded a boat to run away from God! That plan never works for anyone because God is everywhere. He sees all, knows all, and controls all things. Jonah was setting himself up to be disciplined by his heavenly Father. God stirred up a great storm. Then the sailors threw Jonah into the water. To rescue Jonah, God chose a great fish to swallow him. Jonah prayed. God told the fish to spit Jonah out on the dry land.

TALK ABOUT IT

Why didn't Jonah obey God's command to go to Nineveh?

Find as many examples as you can in these chapters of God's power over people, animals, and nature.

Knowing that God is so powerful, how should we respond to the Word of the Lord?

Read Jonah 3–4

What made Jonah so angry? Jonah was angry because God had mercy on Jonah's enemies, the Ninevites. When Jonah warned the Ninevites of God's judgment, a surprising thing happened. The Ninevites repented! This was the last thing Jonah expected to happen. When they repented, God had mercy upon them. God did not destroy them. This made Jonah angry, which shows that Jonah's heart was in a different place than God's heart. The good news of Jesus is all about God's enemies becoming God's friends. Jonah's problem was that he didn't want God's enemies to become God's friends. Jonah wanted them to be destroyed. God's lesson for Jonah is a lesson for us.

TALK ABOUT IT

What was Jonah's sermon to the Ninevites?

How did the Ninevites respond? How did their actions show what was happening in their hearts?

How do you feel when God does something gracious and kind to someone you don't like?

Prayer

God, help us to learn from Jonah's mistakes. Help us to obey Your Word, immediately. And help us to rejoice in the mercy and grace You show to us and to others.

MICAH

Introduction

Micah was a prophet at the same time as Isaiah. Micah's name means "Who is like Yahweh?"

ICEBREAKER: In what city were you born?

Read Micah 5:1–6

What did Micah have to say about Jesus? Micah lived hundreds of years before Jesus came to earth. But God gave Micah something to say about the future when Jesus was born in Bethlehem. In Matthew 2, when Herod asked where the Christ was to be born, the chief priests and scribes answered with these verses from Micah 5. If one of your classmates told you they could predict where a future president was going to be born, would you believe them? Probably not. But God can predict these things because He controls all things. And God revealed many things to His prophets about the coming Messiah. We can read these prophecies in the Old Testament. And we can read how they came to pass in the New Testament.

TALK ABOUT IT

What does Micah say about the One who would be born in Bethlehem? What is He like?

How are Old Testament prophets able to speak about things that would happen hundreds of years later?

How do these verses help you to trust God and worship Him?

Prayer

God, we worship You for Your powerful Word. We praise You that You know all things, even things that haven't happened yet. Thank You for revealing Yourself and Your plans in both the Old Testament and the New Testament. We stand in awe of how this big book, made up of many smaller books, fits together to show us the good news about Jesus.

NAHUM

Introduction

Nahum's name means "comfort." Nahum had a message for Nineveh, a message of judgment and destruction. Nahum's message was not comforting for the people of Nineveh. Rather, his message was comforting to the people of Judah because Nineveh (the capital of the Assyrian Empire) was a harsh enemy of the Israelites.

ICEBREAKER: What are some wrong things that happen in our world that make you angry?

Read Nahum 1:1–8

What else happened in Nineveh? When we hear of the city Nineveh, we think of Jonah. This is the same city where Jonah preached, and the people repented. But now it's a couple generations later, and the people are wicked again. God gave Nahum words to speak against the great city of Nineveh, the capital of the powerful Assyrian Empire. Do we need to be scared of God's wrath? Yes and no. If we're rejecting God and rebelling against Him, we should be scared. God will uphold justice. Those who disobey will be punished. So beware! But if we're trusting in Jesus, and following Him by faith, then our rebellion has been forgiven. Jesus took the punishment for everyone who believes in Him. When we read about God's wrath 1) we should be reminded that God is powerful and just, and 2) we should rejoice that Jesus suffered the wrath of God in our place.

TALK ABOUT IT

What do we learn about God in these verses?

Talk about the fear of the Lord, remembering what Proverbs says about this. How does a knowledge of God's anger against sin connect with our fear of the Lord?

What's the connection between God's wrath and Christ's death?

Prayer

God, we praise You that You are a God of justice. You are not okay with sin. Help us to fear You as we ought. We respect You and want to submit to Your authority in our lives. Thank You that Jesus stood in our place and bore the wrath that we deserve for our sins. You are a God of justice and a God of grace.

HABAKKUK

Introduction

Habakkuk was a prophet to the southern kingdom of Judah, around the same time as Jeremiah. But Habakkuk doesn't speak to the people, like the other prophets. Habakkuk just speaks with God. These conversations between Habakkuk and God remind us of the conversations Job had with God.

ICEBREAKER: Name some things that are hard to wait for.

Read Habakkuk 2:2–20

Habakkuk had questions for God, and God answered him. Habakkuk was confused because it seemed like God was letting evil win. God told Habakkuk to be patient. Wait for it. Wait for God's justice. It will come eventually, in God's perfect timing. We can't see everything now, but "the righteous shall live by his faith" (2:4). And we look forward to the day when the earth will be filled with the knowledge of the glory of the Lord as the waters cover the sea (2:14). These are wonderful truths God revealed to Habakkuk, and they are wonderful truths to encourage us!

When we're confused because it looks like evil is winning in the world, we must look to God and trust in His perfect timing. We must live by faith. And we can rejoice that one day God will make everything right and will fill the earth with the knowledge of His greatness.

TALK ABOUT IT

Do you have questions for God? What are they?

What were Habakkuk's questions for God? How did God answer?

What does it mean to live by faith?

Prayer

God, help us to live by faith. Help us to be patient, and to trust in Your perfect timing. We are eager for the day when Your earth will be filled with the knowledge of Your glory as the waters cover the sea.

ZEPHANIAH

Introduction

Zephaniah was a prophet to the southern kingdom of Judah. His name means "Yahweh has hidden / protected." The first verse of the book gives us not only Zephaniah's name, but also the name of his father and all the way back to his great-great-grandfather.

ICEBREAKER: What is your favorite book of the Bible?

Read Zephaniah 1:1–6; 3:9–20

Remember the young King Josiah? Zephaniah was a prophet during the time of Josiah's reign. Even though Josiah tried very hard to turn the people back to God, judgment was still coming—and coming soon. Zephaniah preached both judgment and hope. This little book begins with scary words about the punishment that will come to those who do not seek the Lord. But the book ends with wonderful promises of God's grace to His people, and God's delight in His people. It's important to understand 1) God's hatred of sin, and 2) God's grace for sinners. Sin makes God very angry. He is not okay with sin. He will punish sin. *And* God is so merciful to provide a way of escape for sinners like you and me. God sent His own beloved Son, Jesus Christ, to be punished instead of us. And since Jesus took the punishment, those who trust in Him receive grace, hope, and joy.

TALK ABOUT IT

Who was king when Zephaniah was a prophet?

What is the emphasis at the start of this book? What is the emphasis at the end?

Explain how God is 1) a God of wrath and 2) a God of grace, both at the same time.

Prayer

God, please help us know You better. Give us a growing motivation to read the Bible and study it because we want to have a closer relationship with You. It is so kind of You to write so many words, so many books, that are part of this big book—the Bible. We praise You that You are a God of justice and wrath, and a God of grace and mercy.

HAGGAI

Introduction

Haggai was a prophet during the time of Ezra, when the people returned to Jerusalem to rebuild the temple.

ICEBREAKER: Talk about some impressive buildings you've seen or visited (for example, a state capitol, a stadium, or a museum).

Read Haggai 1:1–15

Whose house are you building? Are you working hard to get things for yourself? Or are you working hard to build up God's people—the church? Haggai was a prophet during the time of Ezra, when the people returned to Jerusalem to rebuild the temple (see Ezra 5:1; 6:14). The people weren't excited to rebuild the temple. Instead, they were working on their own houses. But then Haggai told them, *Come on, let's get to work on what really matters!* And they did. Today God is building His church all around the world. It's not the physical buildings that are most important. Today God's "house" is the people who are trusting Jesus and following Him. Let's be sure we're giving our best efforts to the building projects that matter most.

TALK ABOUT IT

At first, why weren't the people working to rebuild the house of the Lord?

What did Haggai tell them? What changed?

What are some things you can do to build God's "house"?

Prayer

God, we want to be part of Your building project. You are building up Your people all over the world. Please put us to work, strengthening and expanding Your church.

ZECHARIAH

Introduction

Zechariah was ministering to God's people at the same time as Haggai, when the people returned from exile to rebuild the temple.

ICEBREAKER: Have you ever ridden a donkey or a horse? What was it like?

Read Zechariah 9:9–17

A week before the first Easter, when Jesus entered Jerusalem, what did He ride on? Jesus rode on a donkey. (See Matt. 21:5 and John 12:15, which both quote Zech. 9:9.) Hundreds of years before Jesus came to earth, God gave Zechariah these words that exactly describe something that Jesus would do. What does this teach us about Jesus? It shows us His humility. In His first coming, Jesus came as the suffering servant who went to the cross to die. But at His second coming, Jesus will return like a rider on a war horse (see Rev. 19:11–16). When Jesus comes back, He will come to judge. God's Word teaches us about Jesus in so many ways! Zechariah's prophecy about the Messiah riding a donkey shows us that King Jesus came to us humbly, in righteousness, bringing us salvation.

TALK ABOUT IT

What does Zechariah 9:9 tell us to do at the coming of the king?

What's different between Jesus' first coming and His second coming?

How does this passage lead you to worship Jesus?

Prayer

Jesus, we praise You for being our humble Savior. Thank You for coming down to this earth. Thank You for riding a donkey into Jerusalem, knowing they would crucify You. And thank You that You're coming back to make all things right.

MALACHI

Introduction

Malachi's name means "my messenger." He lived a bit later than Haggai and Zechariah. The people were back in the land, and the temple had been rebuilt. This final book of the Old Testament prepares us for the coming of Jesus, even though it would still be over four hundred years before that would happen.

ICEBREAKER: Imagine what it would be like to introduce a president, or a king or queen. What would you say?

Read Malachi 4:1–6

Here, in the last chapter of the last book of the Old Testament, we have a prophecy about the person who would introduce the Messiah. Malachi 4:5 calls this person "Elijah the prophet." In the New Testament, we learn that John the Baptist is the fulfillment of this prophecy. You can read what the angel told Zechariah in Luke 1:13–17.

After Malachi wrote these words, four hundred years would pass before Jesus was born in Bethlehem. That's a long time to wait! Now we are waiting for the second coming of Jesus. We can see throughout the Scriptures that God has always been faithful to keep His promises.

TALK ABOUT IT

We've heard the phrase "the day of the Lord" from other prophets. When Malachi writes about "the day of the Lord," what is he referring to?

How are Elijah and John the Baptist similar?

Why is it difficult to wait? How can we wait with hope?

Prayer

God, Your Word is amazing! You revealed Yourself in so many ways throughout the Old Testament. Through Your powerful words, and Your mighty works, You showed who You are and Your plan to save people from their sins. Thank You that we can learn so many things about Jesus, even in these books that were written long before Jesus came to earth.

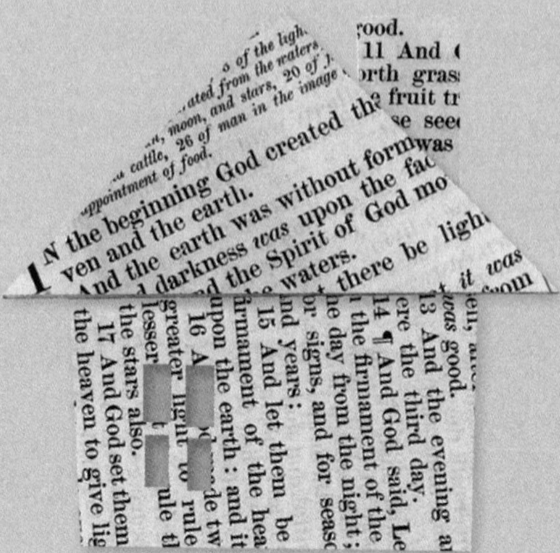

NEW TESTAMENT

THE GOSPELS

Introduction

The word *gospel* means "good news." We use the word gospel to refer to the good news about Jesus. We also use the word *Gospels* to refer to the first four books of the New Testament (the Gospels: Matthew, Mark, Luke, and John) because these books tell us all about the good news of what Jesus has done to save us from our sins. You can think of these books like biographies. They are historically accurate, eyewitness accounts of Jesus' birth, life and ministry, and His death and resurrection.

The first of the Gospels is the book of Matthew. Matthew (aka Levi) was one of the twelve disciples who traveled with Jesus throughout His earthly ministry. Before Matthew met Jesus, he was a tax collector (see Matt. 9:9). Mark (aka John Mark) was a friend of Peter, and Peter was a close disciple of Jesus. Peter shared with Mark about the life and ministry of Jesus, and Mark wrote down what Peter told him. The gospel of Mark is the shortest of the four books and probably written earlier than the others. Luke was a physician and a historian. He was also a missionary companion of the apostle Paul. Luke wrote the gospel of Luke and the book of Acts. John was a close disciple of Jesus, part of the inner circle (along with Peter and James). John also wrote the first, second, and third letters of John and the book of Revelation.

ICEBREAKER: What do you think a miracle is? How would you explain it?

Read Luke 1:5–7, 11–17

What did the angel tell Zechariah? The angel told Zechariah not to be afraid because something wonderful was about to happen. Zechariah and Elizabeth were going to have a baby! Their son would grow up to be like the prophet Elijah (Matt. 11:13–14). God planned for John, later known as John the Baptist, to get people ready to meet God's Son, Jesus. Zechariah and Elizabeth had been married a long time and now their bodies were too old to have a baby. But God made it possible. Only God can make the impossible, possible.

TALK ABOUT IT

What did God do for Zechariah and Elizabeth that was impossible?

What was God's plan for John?

What else has God done that only He can do?

Read Luke 1:26–38

What did the angel tell Mary? The angel told Mary she was going to be the mother of Jesus. This was good news. The people had waited a long time for the Messiah King God promised to send. But Mary knew it was not possible for her to have a baby. Mary was a virgin; she and Joseph were not married yet. The angel Gabriel said the Holy Spirit would make the impossible, possible. God would make the life of Jesus begin in Mary. Joseph would be a father to Jesus on earth. But God is Jesus' Father.

TALK ABOUT IT

What did God do for Mary that was impossible?

Who would be Jesus' father?

Why do you think we need to know that only God could be Jesus' Father?

Prayer

Lord, You are the God of the impossible. I praise You for Your omnipotence and Your sovereign plan. Thank You for the amazing gift of the virgin birth and Your plan of bringing Jesus to earth as a baby. Help me to trust You for the impossible in my life. Give me a humble faith like Mary.

Read Matthew 1:18–20

Who were Jesus' mother and father? Jesus' mother was Mary. When Mary wondered how she would give birth to a child when she did not have a husband, the angel said, "The Holy Spirit will come upon you, and the power of the Most High will overshadow you" (Luke 1:35). The Holy Spirit created the life of Jesus in Mary's body. Joseph later became Mary's husband, but God is Jesus' Father. God sent His Son into the world as a baby. Jesus is God and man. God gave Mary and Joseph faith to believe His Word.

TALK ABOUT IT

Who were Jesus' mother and father?

How did God show Mary and Joseph what was about to happen?

What questions do you have about Jesus' birth?

Read Matthew 1:21–25

What does the name Jesus mean? The name Jesus means "God is salvation." Jesus Christ came "to save His people from their sins" (v. 21). The word *saved* tells us that the person who does not belong to Jesus is lost. Jesus told the people that if they did not believe in Him, it was a sin against God. Jesus takes the sins of those who trust Him and saves them from the righteous judgment of God. The name *Jesus* means Jesus saves us from sin, and the name *Immanuel* means Jesus is "God with us" (v. 23). Jesus lives in the life of the believer and lets us know God.

TALK ABOUT IT

What does it mean to be lost?

What does it mean to be saved?

In what ways is Jesus "God with us"?

Prayer

God, we praise You for Immanuel, God with us. Thank You for the gift of Jesus to save Your people from their sins. Thank You that everyone who trusts in You and calls on Your name will be saved. Help us to see our sin and turn away from it, rejoicing that we are saved by Your grace alone.

Read Luke 1:39–45

What happened when Elizabeth saw Mary? The baby inside Elizabeth's body jumped when Mary spoke. The baby was John. The Holy Spirit helped John and Elizabeth know that Mary was the mother of Jesus. The Holy Spirit makes it possible for us to understand God's truth. Mary and Elizabeth were so happy that God loved them. God loved them so much that He would send His Son to make the impossible, possible. They could not save themselves, but Jesus would save them from their sin. God forgives all those who believe the truth about His Son, Jesus.

TALK ABOUT IT

What did the Holy Spirit help John and Elizabeth know?

What was impossible for Mary and Elizabeth to do for themselves?

What does God make possible for everyone who believe in Jesus?

Prayer

Heavenly Father, everything about Jesus' birth was a miracle. Only You have power to make the impossible, possible. I need You to do the impossible in my life too. Even on my best days, I have sin in my heart. Please give me faith to believe the truth about Jesus. Please forgive me and make me Your child.

Read Luke 1:46–56

What was Mary's song about? Mary sang about God as her Savior. Mary knew God did not choose her to be Jesus' mother because of anything she had done or who she was. She had sin in her heart just like everyone else. God does not choose someone because of what they will do for Him. He chooses people because of what He will do for them. Mary needed a Savior as we all do (Isa. 53:6). God gave Mary the gift of forgiveness. This forgiveness came through Jesus. Jesus saves His children from their sin.

TALK ABOUT IT

Why did God choose Mary to be Jesus' mother?

What did God do for Mary?

What do you need God to do for you?

Read Luke 1:57–66

Why were the people amazed that Zechariah wrote "John" on the tablet? They knew only God could have changed Zechariah's mind and heart. From the time Zechariah was a boy, he knew about God. His parents taught him to pray and read God's Word. But Zechariah doubted the angel Gabriel's message. Like Zechariah, we can do good things, yet sometimes doubt God and His Word. To trust God means to believe God and His plan for sending Jesus. It means to ask God to help you turn away from sin and love Him with your whole heart. God changes our heart to trust in Him.

TALK ABOUT IT

What did God do for Zechariah?

In what specific ways do we see Elizabeth's and Zechariah's faith in these verses?

What does it mean to trust God?

Read Luke 2:1–7

God said Jesus would be born in Bethlehem (Mic. 5:2). But Mary and Joseph lived in Nazareth. Nazareth is far away from Bethlehem. At the time of Jesus' birth, Caesar Augustus made a plan to count all the people in his land. Then Caesar would know who owed him tax money. But God had another plan (Prov. 16:9). To be counted, each family had to go to their family's hometown. Joseph was from the family line of King David and had to go to Bethlehem. God's plans always happen.

TALK ABOUT IT

How did God plan to get Mary and Joseph to Bethlehem?

What does it mean that God's plans always happen?

How do you see God working out His plan in your life?

Read Luke 2:8–14

God gave angels the special job of telling people Jesus was coming. On the night Jesus was born, God sent an angel to tell the shepherds. The brightness of God was all around the angel. Then the angel spoke the best news anyone had ever heard—the Savior had been born. The angels in heaven could not hold back their joy any longer. Suddenly thousands and thousands of angels burst through the dark sky. They praised God for sending Jesus. Through Jesus, God made a way for people to come to Him.

TALK ABOUT IT

What did the angels tell the shepherds about God's plan?

For what did the angels praise God?

What can you praise God for today?

Read Luke 2:15–20

Why were the shepherds the first to hear about Jesus' birth? Shepherds were usually the last to hear important news. A king coming to a city would never go out to see the shepherds. Yet God's love does not depend on how strong or smart a person is. God does not love a person when they can play the piano better than someone else or do more work at church than others. God does not invite only those who are good enough. God sent Jesus before we did anything to deserve His love. God invites all to come to Jesus.

TALK ABOUT IT

Why do you think the shepherds were the first to get an invitation to come to Jesus?

What was their reaction?

What are some things people think can earn God's love? Why are they wrong to think so?

Prayer

Father God, You are full of love and mercy. I feel like the last one who deserves to hear the good news about Jesus. Yet, in Your kindness, You have told me about Him. I want to come to Jesus and know Him as my Savior.

Please help me to praise You for the great gift of Jesus. I want to have the same joy that the angels had the night Jesus was born.

Read John 1:1–18

Who is Jesus? Read John 1:1–5 again and this time read "Jesus" instead of "the Word." Jesus is with God and, at the same time, Jesus is God. There is God the Father, God the Son, and God the Holy Spirit. There is One God who is three Persons. Jesus is not only a man, Jesus is God. In God's power, Jesus created the earth and everything in it. Jesus created every star in the sky as well as the mountains and oceans. Jesus is the Word. He is with God, and He is God.

When was Jesus born? Your birthday is the celebration of the first day of your life. Jesus' birthday was the first day of His life on earth, but it was not the first day of His life. Jesus has always been alive. Long before Jesus created the stars, sun, moon and earth, He was alive. Jesus has always been alive and will be alive forever.

TALK ABOUT IT

Who is Jesus?

When was Jesus born?

Why did Jesus come to live on earth?

Prayer

Lord, we praise You that even though Jesus' birthday is a celebration of His first day of life on earth, Jesus has always been alive. Thank You for the Trinity: God the Father, God the Son, and God the Holy Spirit. You are always with us and leading us. Help us to follow You in all that we say and do.

Read Matthew 2:1–12

Why did the wise men call Jesus King of the Jews? They called Jesus King of the Jews because Jesus is the Messiah King who God promised to send. These wise men were from Persia. They were men who studied the stars, and when they saw this bright star in the sky they believed it meant the great Messiah King of the Jewish people had come. They left their home in Persia to follow this star. The star showed them the way to King Jesus. They wanted to worship the King Jesus and give Him gifts.

TALK ABOUT IT

Why did the wise men call Jesus King of the Jews?

Why did they want to find Jesus?

What gifts do you have that you can offer to Jesus, as an act of worship?

Read Luke 2:21–35

Simeon waited a long time to see Jesus. The Holy Spirit told Simeon he would not die before he saw Jesus. Through the Holy Spirit, we are able to hear and understand God and desire to please Him. With the Holy Spirit's help, we are able to love and obey God. Simeon knew God sent Jesus as the Savior of all who ask for His forgiveness. Jesus came to forgive people of every nation and language. When we place our trust in Jesus Christ, God gives us His Holy Spirit. The Holy Spirit enables God's children to obey God.

TALK ABOUT IT

Who told Simeon he would not die before he saw Jesus?

What did Simeon understand about baby Jesus?

What does God give to us when we trust in Jesus?

Read Luke 2:36–40

Anna also waited a long time to see Jesus. Anna loved God and believed His promise to send Jesus. Anna knew God would send Jesus as our Savior. Anna prayed every day that God would send Jesus. Prayer is talking with God. God always hears the prayers of His children and answers with what we need at the right time. Finally, the day came when the Savior she had prayed for was right there in front of her. How did Anna know what to pray? The Bible shows us what to pray for and the Holy Spirit teaches us to pray.

TALK ABOUT IT

What is prayer?

How did Anna know what to pray?

What will you talk with God about today?

Read Luke 2:41–52

Like other babies, Jesus learned to talk and walk. He grew from a child to a man, like any other boy. He loved his brothers and sisters and obeyed his parents. Jesus perfectly obeyed God's law from the day He was born to the day He died. As a child and as a man, Jesus was tempted to sin. Jesus understands us and can help us. The Holy Spirit gave Him strength to obey God fully. Jesus overcame every type of temptation we face with the gifts God gives every believer: God's Word, prayer, and the Holy Spirit.

TALK ABOUT IT

When you think about Jesus growing up, what surprises you?

Why does Jesus understand you and how can He help you?

How are you tempted to disobey? Will you ask God for help?

Prayer

Father God, thank You for Your Word and Holy Spirit. Jesus, thank You for understanding my struggle with obedience. Even when I obey my parents and act loving to my family my heart is often angry. Please help me remember to call upon You when I am tempted. Help me to depend on Your Word and Holy Spirit to live for You.

Read Matthew 3:1–6

Who was John the Baptist? John was the son promised to Zechariah and Elizabeth and also the man God chose to tell people about Jesus. People thought Jesus was just a carpenter. God wanted people to know Jesus is His Son, the Messiah. God wants people to know the truth about Jesus. So God chose John to tell the people to get ready to meet Jesus. John did not live in a house, wear fancy clothes, or eat delicious food. And John baptized people in the Jordan River, which is why he was known as John the Baptist.

TALK ABOUT IT

Who was John the Baptist?

What did God want people to know about Jesus?

Who does God want you to tell about Jesus?

Read Matthew 3:7–12

What did John tell the people to do? John told the people to get ready for Jesus and to repent. To repent means to turn away from sin and turn to God. Many people were baptized by John to show they were sorry for their sin. They believed their sins could be forgiven through Jesus. There were other people who did not believe what John said. They believed God already forgave their sins because they were from the family line of Abraham. They were wrong and John called them snakes. Our sin matters to God, and He sent Jesus to take away our sin.

TALK ABOUT IT

What does it mean to repent?

Why did some people not believe what John said about Jesus?

What sins do you need to repent of and ask Jesus to forgive?

Read Matthew 3:13–17

What did Jesus want John to do? Jesus told John to baptize Him. John was surprised because he knew Jesus did not need to be baptized. Jesus had never done anything wrong and did not need to repent of any sin. But Jesus said it was right for John to baptize Him. Jesus wanted to obey all of God's plans. As Jesus came up from the water God's Holy Spirit came down like a dove and landed on Jesus. Then God said, "This is my beloved Son, with whom I am well pleased" (v. 17). Jesus is the Savior God promised to send.

TALK ABOUT IT

Why was John surprised that Jesus wanted to be baptized?

What did God say when Jesus came up from the water?

Who is Jesus and what does this mean to you?

Read Matthew 4:1–4

Why did God let Jesus be tempted? God let Jesus be tempted to show that Jesus is our Messiah King, the One God promised to send. God wants us to know that the devil tempted Jesus. Jesus was tempted in every way we are, but He never sinned. It was because Jesus never sinned that He could take the punishment for our sin in our place. You can trust Jesus for the forgiveness of your sin. We are all tempted to do what God doesn't want us to do. We are tempted to speak words that are unkind, take what does not belong to us, and lie to our parents. To be tempted is not a sin. It is sin when we give in to the temptation and do what is wrong. Jesus is able to help us when we are tempted.

TALK ABOUT IT

What does it mean to be tempted?

Why did God let Jesus be tempted?

Why is it not a sin to be tempted?

Read Matthew 4:5–11

How did Jesus resist temptation? Jesus resisted temptation with the power of God and the truth of God's Word. Jesus' temptation was harder than anyone's temptation will ever be. He knows how hard it is for us to do what God wants and to not sin. Jesus helps us resist temptation in the same way He did—with the power of God and the truth of His Word. He can help us when we are tempted. When you are tempted to sin, call to Jesus for help, and He will give you power not to sin. Jesus loves you and cares for you.

TALK ABOUT IT

How did Jesus resist temptation?

How does Jesus help us not to sin when we are tempted?

For what temptation will you ask for Jesus' help?

Prayer

Lord Jesus, we praise You that You were tempted but did not sin. You set an example for us in fighting sin through using the truth of God's Word. Help us not to give in to temptation and remind us that You will never let us be tempted beyond our ability but will provide a way of escape (1 Cor. 10:13).

Read Mark 1:16–20

What did Jesus tell the fishermen? Jesus told them to follow Him. Jesus would send them out to fish for people. Instead of feeding people fish, they would feed them the truth about Jesus. Jesus is the King of God's kingdom. Jesus came to live for us and die for us. He rose from the dead and is now on His throne in heaven, ruling over the universe. Knowing Jesus is King fills our hearts with true joy. Food makes us feel full for a little while, but Jesus makes us feel satisfied forever. Jesus is the One to follow.

TALK ABOUT IT

What did Jesus tell the fishermen to do?

What is the truth about Jesus?

Why does following Jesus fill us with true joy?

Prayer

God, thank You for sending Jesus. And Jesus, thank You for living for me and dying for me. Please give me faith to trust in You Jesus. I want to follow You.

Read John 3:1–8

Who was Nicodemus? Nicodemus was a wealthy, well-known man, a Pharisee and a member of the Jewish ruling council, the Sanhedrin.

Even though Nicodemus studied the Scriptures, he was not sure if he was in God's family.

To be in God's family, Nicodemus needed a new heart, so he could love God. He went to Jesus for answers. Jesus told Nicodemus he must be "born again." What a surprise this must have been to Nicodemus! What does it mean to be "born again"? To be "born again" is to be created all over again—on the inside—to be born into God's family. When we are born again, God gives us His Holy Spirit to create in us a spiritual heart that loves and trusts Jesus as Savior. You cannot see the Holy Spirit—Jesus said the Holy Spirit is like the wind—but you know when He gives this new life to you.

TALK ABOUT IT

Who was Nicodemus?

What does it mean to be born again?

Have you been born again?

Read Mark 6:1–6

Why was Jesus amazed? Jesus was amazed that people in His hometown did not believe in Him. They knew Jesus' teaching was from God. They knew Jesus' power was from God. But they decided not to believe He was the Messiah that God promised to send. They thought the Messiah should be someone different. Jesus was someone they remembered as a simple carpenter. Jesus came to them with truth, but they refused to believe. Many people want Jesus to be different than He is. Unbelief does not change the truth about Jesus. Jesus is the Messiah.

TALK ABOUT IT

Why was Jesus amazed that the people in His hometown did not believe in Him?

Why do many people refuse to believe the truth about Jesus?

Do you know someone who wants Jesus to be different than He really is? Encourage them to know the Jesus of the Bible.

Read Mark 6:7–13

What did Jesus want His disciples to do? Jesus wanted His disciples to learn to go out and tell others the truth about Him. They would learn that even though Jesus came to give us the best news in the world, many people refuse to believe Him. People would refuse to believe His disciples too. Even though Jesus has power over our worst enemy, Satan, people hate Him. People would hate His disciples too. Jesus' disciples would learn that following Him is hard and also joyful. God gives us everything we need to follow Jesus.

TALK ABOUT IT

What did Jesus want His disciples to learn?

When have you learned that not all people want to hear the truth about Jesus?

If you are Jesus' disciple, what is He teaching you about telling others the truth about Him?

Read Luke 5:17–26

Why did Jesus tell the paralyzed man his sins were forgiven? Jesus knew the sin in the man's heart was worse than being paralyzed. But the teachers of the law did not like it when Jesus talked about sin. They knew only God can forgive sin. Jesus has the power to forgive sin because He is God. Jesus saw their hearts and knew they did not believe this. But Jesus knew the paralyzed man and his friends believed in Him. Jesus is the Messiah that God promised to send.

TALK ABOUT IT

How did the friends of the paralyzed man get him to Jesus?

What did Jesus know was worse than being paralyzed?

Why is Jesus able to forgive sin?

Read Luke 7:1–10

What did Jesus say about the centurion? Jesus said the centurion was a man of great faith. That means the centurion trusted Jesus and knew Jesus had the power of God to heal his sick servant. God's power is so great that He created the universe from nothing. Without God's power everything would fall apart. His power holds the stars in the sky. God's power keeps our hearts beating and our lungs breathing every day of our life. Even death is not stronger than God. When God's children die, they will have a life with Him that does not end.

TALK ABOUT IT

Why did Jesus say the centurion was a man of great faith?

Why can God promise His children life with Him that does not end?

What would Jesus say about your trust in Him?

Read Luke 7:11–17

What did Jesus say to the widow? Jesus told her not to cry. He loved her and gave life back to her son. Jesus has power over death. After Jesus died on the cross and was buried in the tomb, He came back to life three days later. Jesus died and rose again for us. We do not need to live apart from God forever. Jesus has the power to give us the best life of all—life with God in heaven forever. We will all die, but all who trust Jesus as Savior live with Him for eternity (John 11:25–26).

TALK ABOUT IT

Why could Jesus promise to give life back to the dead?

Why did Jesus die and rise again?

Who will live with God forever in heaven?

Read Matthew 13:1–9

What story did Jesus tell about soil? The story is about a farmer planting seeds in the soil. Jesus wants us to know that God's Word is like a seed, and our hearts are like the soil. In Jesus' story, not every seed grows. The soil on the path was hard, so birds came and ate the seeds. Other soil was full of rocks. Because the seeds could not grow deep roots, they sprouted quickly. But the sun killed them. Other soil was full of thorns that crowded out the seeds. But when the seeds fell on good soil they grew and produced a large crop.

TALK ABOUT IT

What were the different kinds of soil in Jesus' story?

What does Jesus want us to know about the seed and the soil?

How is your love for God and His Word growing?

Read Matthew 13:10–17

What is a parable? A parable is a story that teaches us an important truth about God's kingdom. Jesus' parables help God's children know

Him better. But parables are not easy to understand. Those who are not God's children do not understand, and they do not ask for God's help. We need more than our minds to understand God's Word. We need God's Spirit to reveal His truth to our hearts. God's children may struggle to understand the Bible, but hard truths are actually God's gift. In the struggle, we learn His Holy Spirit helps us. The more the Holy Spirit helps us understand, the more our love for God grows.

TALK ABOUT IT

What is a parable?

Why are many people blind to spiritual truth?

How is it possible for God's children to understand hard truths in the Bible?

Read Matthew 13:18–23

What does the parable about the soil mean? The farmer is someone who tells the good news about Jesus (Luke 8:11). Hard soil is like a person who does not want to hear the truth about God. Rocky soil is like a person who at first is happy to hear God's Word. Then when a difficult thing happens to them, they stop listening to God. The thorny soil is like a person who thinks that things can make them happier than God. The good soil is like a person who hears God's Word and believes the truth about Jesus. Jesus is able to make even the hardest heart into good soil.

TALK ABOUT IT

Who is the farmer in the parable about the soil?

What happens in the life of someone whose heart is like good soil?

What is the soil of your heart like—hard, rocky, thorny, or good?

Read John 6:1–14, 35–40

Why did Jesus come down from heaven? Jesus is God and He came down from heaven to give spiritual life to all who receive Him. To receive Jesus means to believe He came to forgive your sin and give you eternal life. To receive Jesus means to love Him as your Savior. When you receive bread into your stomach, it gives life to your body. When you receive Jesus into your mind and heart, He gives you spiritual life. The best fullness we can have is to be filled with Jesus. Even when our body dies one day, our spirit will live with God forever.

TALK ABOUT IT

How did Jesus' miracle teach us something about who He is and His mission?

What does it mean that Jesus is the Bread of Life?

What does it mean to receive Jesus?

Read Mark 8:27–30

Why did Jesus ask His disciples to say who He is? Jesus wanted His disciples to commit their lives to Him. Did they believe He was more than a good teacher or prophet? Peter boldly said, "You are the Christ" (v. 29). Peter knew Jesus was not just a man, He is truly God. It was not Peter's smart thinking or desire to do good things that helped him understand this truth. To know Jesus as our King is a gift from God. Those who know Jesus declare who He is and commit their lives to Him.

TALK ABOUT IT

What were people saying about Jesus?

What did the disciples need to know about Jesus?

What does it mean that Jesus is the Christ?

Read Mark 8:31–33

Why did Jesus speak to Satan when He was talking to Peter? Jesus took Peter's words of rejection of the cross as coming from Satan. Satan tempted Jesus to avoid the cross, many times. The cross would be painful and shameful for Jesus. And the experience of carrying His people's sins would be the greatest pain of all. But Jesus came into the world to pay for our sin with His life. Peter failed to give his mind to God and think about God's plans. Instead, he gave his feelings over to Satan. As with Peter, Satan tempts us to think about Jesus' cross as strange, cruel, and unnecessary.

TALK ABOUT IT

Who tempted Jesus to avoid the cross?

Why did Peter reject Jesus' teaching about the cross?

What is your reaction to the cross?

Read Mark 8:34–38

What does it mean to follow Jesus? Jesus said it means to take up your cross. This means to do the Father's will for your life, as Jesus did. It means not thinking of your desires, feelings, plans, and rights first. Instead of yourself, you choose God's thoughts and God's will first. We discover God's thoughts and His will through prayer and reading the Bible. God's Word teaches us how to make choices at school or with friends based on God's will, not on what we think will make us happy. It may seem that you lose what you want most, yet by following Jesus, you will find joy and fulfillment.

TALK ABOUT IT

What does it mean to take up your cross?

How do we discover God's thoughts and His will?

As a believer in Jesus, when have you had to make a choice to follow Him instead of your friends?

Prayer

Lord, we praise You for being obedient to the Father's will. You lived a perfect life, suffered, and died on a cross so that we could be free from our sin. Help us to take up our cross and live a life that is pleasing to You. Help us to be willing to suffer or do hard things, knowing that following You will give us more joy than anything else.

Read Mark 9:14–19

Why did Jesus speak so strongly to the people? Jesus was warning the people. They had come to see miracles but failed to believe in Him. The time given to believe in Jesus is not unlimited. Jesus' disciples failed to help the boy even though He had given them power to deliver people from demons and disease. They had experienced God's power working through them. This time they failed. Had they begun to act as though the power belonged to them? Did the disciples start to rely on their own abilities instead of God's? They needed to learn what faith means. Faith means confessing that Jesus is the rescuer. Faith also means relying on Jesus to accomplish His will.

TALK ABOUT IT

What warning did Jesus give the people?

What did the disciples need to learn about faith?

In what situation have you started to rely on your abilities instead of God's?

Read Luke 10:25–37

Why did the lawyer want to justify himself? The lawyer wanted to think that he was keeping all of God's commands. But that's not possible for sinful humans. We all fall short. What does Jesus' story teach us about keeping God's commands? It teaches us that keeping God's commands is more difficult than we might think. Samaritans and Jews did not like each other. They were not friends. The lawyer thought he was keeping God's command to love his neighbors. But he didn't think he needed to love Samaritans. Jesus' story about the good Samaritan would have been shocking for the Jewish lawyer to hear.

TALK ABOUT IT

What question did the lawyer have for Jesus?

What does Jesus' story teach us?

How is Jesus a good Samaritan to us?

Read Luke 12:13–21

What did the rich man treasure? The man treasured—or loved—money because he believed that things could make him happy. The man used up all the days of his life getting more and more stuff. Jesus called the man a fool. The happy feeling of buying what we want does not last. Things wear out or break, or we lose interest in them. Even the best gift cannot make our hearts happy forever. God made us, so He is our greatest and lasting happiness. When we know God, love Him, enjoy Him, and glorify Him, we are truly happy.

TALK ABOUT IT

Why did Jesus call the man a fool?

What is the truth about our stuff?

What is the only way for us to be truly happy?

Read Luke 12:22–29

What treasure did the disciples want? They wanted food, clothes and health. That's not wrong, but Jesus warns us not to worry about having enough. We work for our daily needs. But our loving heavenly Father takes care of us. If our God takes care of the birds and flowers, He will take care of us. Money, good grades, a place on the team, or a part in the school play are important but will never completely make us truly happy. Even friendship does not satisfy if we only want to be popular. True happiness comes in knowing and loving God.

TALK ABOUT IT

What treasure does Jesus warn us not to worry about?

What are some things that people hope will make them happy?

Where do we find true happiness?

Prayer

Heavenly Father, we praise You that You know what we need even before we ask. You provide everything we need, just as You care for the birds and the flowers. Thank You for seeing us and caring for us. Help us to not worry about tomorrow, but to turn our eyes to seek Your kingdom first. You are our greatest treasure.

Read Luke 12:30–34

What is the greatest treasure? Jesus is the greatest treasure and king! King Jesus bought us with His blood which is more valuable than gold. Only Jesus can make our lives in this world, truly happy. And His forever life in heaven is the amazing gift only He can give. This treasure belongs to those who trust Jesus as their Savior and King. This treasure grows as we read God's Word, pray, obey God, and use our money and talents to help other people know Jesus. Jesus is our greatest treasure.

TALK ABOUT IT

What makes Jesus our greatest treasure?

What lesser treasure will you put aside to spend time with God?

How might you use your money or talents to help someone else know Jesus' love?

Read Luke 13:10–17

Why was the synagogue ruler angry? The synagogue ruler was angry because Jesus didn't follow all their rules. The Sabbath was God's special day for His children. God knew it would make them happy to have a day to think about Him and talk with Him. But many rules had made the Sabbath hard instead of happy. Jesus set the woman free from Satan's power. She stood up straight after bending over for eighteen years. The synagogue ruler cared more about his rules than he did about the people. God loves us and wants us to know Him.

TALK ABOUT IT

What did Jesus do for the woman?

How did the synagogue ruler react to Jesus?

Why did God give the Sabbath day to His children?

Read Luke 14:25–33

What does it mean to be Jesus' disciple? Jesus did not mean children must hate their parents. Jesus wants children to love and obey their parents (Eph. 6:1–3). But Jesus must be first in our hearts. What does it cost to follow Jesus? We do not pay anything to follow Jesus just like you do not pay to be part of your family. But there is a cost. There are things in this world we will need to give up in order to follow Jesus with our whole heart. Jesus' true disciples learn that their hearts are most happy when they love Jesus and do whatever He says. Jesus' disciples receive much more from Him than anything they give up.

TALK ABOUT IT

What does it cost to be part of your family?

What does it cost you to follow Jesus?

What has Jesus given you that is much greater than anything you have given up to follow Him?

Read Luke 18:9–14

Why did Jesus tell this story? Jesus wants us to know that God does not play favorites. God rescues people who have families in church and people who do not. He saves people who are rich and those who are poor. He saves people who are smart and those who are not smart. The Pharisee (religious leader) thanked God that he was better than others. He did not think he needed God's forgiveness. The tax collector knew he did not deserve God's love. He depended on God's mercy. God forgives all who turn from sin and trust in Jesus.

TALK ABOUT IT

Why did Jesus tell this story?

What did the tax collector know about himself?

What have you learned about God's forgiveness?

Read Luke 18:15–17

What does it look like to depend on God? Jesus showed us. He called the little children to come to him. Little children cannot work. They cannot earn their food and clothing. They depend on their Mom and Dad to provide everything—to love them, comfort them, and teach them. God's children don't tell God what they will do for Him. They depend on God for all their needs. Jesus invites us to admit our biggest need is for God's love and forgiveness. God's children depend on God's love and forgiveness.[1]

TALK ABOUT IT

How did Jesus teach the people about humility?

What do you learn about God in these verses?

How will you depend on God today?

Read John 8:31–41

Why do we need to be set free? Jesus said we need to be set free because we are slaves. We may feel free, but we are not. We are slaves to sin, until Jesus rescues us. Jesus wants us to know that sin is our worst problem. How does Jesus set us free? Jesus sets us free from our slave owner, the devil, by His power and strength and truth. He brings us out of captivity to the lies of the devil and into the freedom and light of knowing His truth. We can read Jesus' words, and abide in His truth, by reading the Bible.

TALK ABOUT IT

Why do we need to be set free?

What's the difference between a slave and a son?

Is there a sin you feel enslaved to? How can God's truth give you freedom?

Read Luke 18:18–30

What did Jesus want this man to know? Only God is perfectly good. The wealthy ruler knew Jesus was a good teacher. But Jesus is more than a good teacher. Jesus never sinned. Only Jesus kept God's commandments perfectly. Jesus is God. Jesus sees our hearts and loves us. He knows our greatest need is to trust him. Jesus told the man to give away what he trusted most–his money. Jesus does not tell everyone to give away all their money. Jesus reveals whatever sin keeps us from knowing, loving, and trusting God.[2]

TALK ABOUT IT

Why did the man go away sad?

How does Jesus give more joy than anything money can buy?

Is there an earthly treasure you're clinging to that is keeping you from following Jesus?

Read John 10:1–18

There are many shepherds, but only Jesus is the Good Shepherd. What makes Jesus different? Other shepherds or people who were paid to care for the sheep may look like good shepherds. But when the wolf comes, they leave the sheep and run away. The wolf can attack the sheep because the shepherd cares more about himself than the sheep. It is Jesus, the Good Shepherd, who lays down His life for His sheep. Jesus gave His life for us to enter God's family. Why did Jesus have to die? Death is the punishment for sin. Jesus died in our place, taking the punishment for our sin. When you receive Jesus as your Savior, you belong to Jesus and are one of His sheep. No one can take you from God's family. Jesus is the Good Shepherd who protects and leads His sheep. Jesus knows His children by name. His children love Him and follow Him.

TALK ABOUT IT

What makes Jesus such a good shepherd?

Why did Jesus have to die for us to enter God's family?

In what ways are you listening to the voice of the Good Shepherd?

Read John 11:1–44

Who was Lazarus? Lazarus was the brother of Mary and Martha. Lazarus, Mary, and Martha were good friends of Jesus. They believed in Him and loved Him very much. Jesus loved them too. Why did Jesus not come to help Lazarus before he died? Jesus told His friends there was a reason for Lazarus' sickness. Lazarus' sickness and death would glorify Jesus. His death would show that Jesus has the same attributes as God. People would see Jesus could raise Lazarus from the dead and know He is God. Death is real for us, just as it was for Lazarus. And death is sad. Even though Jesus knew He would raise Lazarus from the dead, He was sad. The sadness in Jesus' heart over Lazarus' death made Him cry. But death is not the end for God's children. Jesus prayed and Lazarus was raised from the dead. Jesus has the power to give eternal life to all who believe in Him.

TALK ABOUT IT

Why didn't Jesus go immediately to help Lazarus?

How did Jesus feel about Lazarus' death?

What does Jesus give to all who believe in Him?

Read Matthew 18:21–27

What is the kingdom of God like? Jesus said the kingdom of God is like a king with servants who owe him money. The servants' debt is great and their penalty is severe. Jesus says God is like this king and all people are like the servants. Every sinful thought and action makes our debt greater. We could do good things every day and our debt would only increase. The penalty for our sin is severe. God's mercy is so great that He does not give His children the consequence they deserve. He sent Jesus to take our penalty for sin and die in our place.

TALK ABOUT IT

What is the kingdom of God like?

How great is our sin and our penalty for sin?

What difference has God's mercy made for you?

Read Matthew 18:28–35

What did the servant do? The servant went home, but the king's mercy had not changed his heart. The amount the king had forgiven the servant was more than he could have paid in a thousand years. The servant went to a friend who owed him a small amount. He refused to give his friend time to pay and sent him to prison. The other servants saw how wrong this was and told the king. The king called the servant wicked. God's children forgive others because they know God has forgiven them. God has changed His children's hearts, so they know He will help them forgive others when they ask.

TALK ABOUT IT

What did the servant do when he got home?

Why do God's children forgive others?

When have you asked God to help you forgive someone?

Read Luke 19:1–10

Why did Jesus go to Jericho? Jesus went to Jericho to find Zacchaeus. He knew Zacchaeus was lost. What does it mean to be lost? Without Jesus we are all lost. Zacchaeus thought money was the way to happiness. But then he heard Jesus was coming to town. He even climbed a tree to see over the crowd. Zacchaeus opened his home and heart to Jesus. Zacchaeus had thought money would fill his heart with happiness. Then he discovered that knowing Jesus filled his empty heart with a greater happiness than he had ever known. Zacchaeus decided to turn away from lying and cheating. He decided to give his money to the poor and pay back all the people he had cheated.

TALK ABOUT IT

Why did Jesus go to Jericho?

How would you describe what it means to be "lost" without Jesus?

What does it mean to you to know that Jesus loves you?

Read Matthew 20:1–16

What can God's children know about God's kingdom? God invites all kinds of people into His kingdom, no matter how good or bad they have been. The workers who worked all day were angry when the farmer paid the last workers a full day's pay. They were not grateful for the farmer's kindness. We are like those workers when we do not like God's generosity to someone we do not think deserves it. When we understand how great and how kind God is, we can be happy when He is kind to others.

TALK ABOUT IT

Why were the workers who worked all day angry?

How are we sometimes like the angry workers?

When have you been happy about God's kindness to someone you know?

Read Mark 10:32–34

Why did Jesus go to Jerusalem to be killed? Jesus knew He came to save His people from their sins. That meant He had to die. Jesus knew everything that would happen to Him. No one knows the future except God, and Jesus is God. Jesus knew every detail of His death. God the Father planned it and Jesus fulfilled it. He was born to be the Savior and that meant suffering and death. Jesus walked ahead of everyone to Jerusalem, and the disciples were amazed. Why was He walking into danger? Jesus knew He came to save His people from their sins. Jesus wanted to die and rise again to save His people.

TALK ABOUT IT

What did Jesus know would happen in Jerusalem?

Why did He tell His disciples repeatedly about this? See also Mark 8:31 and 9:30–32.

How does it make you feel that Jesus knew ahead of time what was going to happen to Him?

Read Mark 10:35–45

Why were James and John so bold with Jesus? They thought true happiness meant to rule with Jesus, in the two highest positions in His kingdom. They liked the idea of ruling with Jesus. But it was hard to think about the cross and what that meant for them. Only Jesus could take the "cup" and "baptism" of judgment for our sins. But to follow Jesus means to embrace the suffering that comes with denying ourselves. The disciples thought greatness meant having others serve them. But Jesus taught that greatness is serving others.

TALK ABOUT IT

Why was it hard for the disciples to think about the cross?

What does it mean to follow Jesus?

When has God given you an opportunity to serve others?

Read John 13:1–17

What did Jesus do before He died? Jesus washed His friends' feet to teach them to serve each other. In those days, it was the job of a servant to wash people's feet when they came into the house. People wore sandals and their feet got covered with dirt from the road whenever they walked outside. Jesus' friends were amazed that Jesus did not ask a servant to wash their feet. Jesus was their leader and most leaders want to be served. Most leaders like to be praised for what they do. Servants help others and do not expect to be praised for what they do. Those who are saved by Jesus serve others. To serve means we help others and want them to praise Jesus instead of us.

TALK ABOUT IT

What did Jesus know?

Why didn't Peter want Jesus to wash his feet?

What does Jesus' example teach us?

Read Mark 14:10–21

What did Jesus know about Judas? Jesus knew Judas had already decided to betray Him. Judas had heard Jesus teach and watched Him heal the sick. But Judas listened to his own rebellious heart and Satan's temptations. Judas must have been a great actor because the other disciples did not know of his plans. We, too, may fool people close to us into thinking we believe in Jesus. Jesus calls us to be honest with Him, so He can forgive us and change us. Jesus knew about the betrayal, and Judas' plans could not stop God's plan.

TALK ABOUT IT

What did the chief priests give to Judas? Why?

When Jesus said to the disciples, "one of you will betray me" (v. 18), how did they respond?

How had Judas fooled everyone but Jesus?

Read Mark 14:27–31

What did Jesus know about Peter? Jesus knew from the prophet Zechariah that Peter and all the disciples would fail to stay with Him at the cross. The disciples would be so disappointed in their failure. Peter did not ever think he would be weak and fail to stand for Jesus. Peter did not want to listen to Jesus' warning about his weakness. Later when the disciples remembered that Jesus knew of their weakness, the pain would ease. Jesus' promise to meet Peter in Galilee must have also been a great comfort. Jesus warns us of our weaknesses and promises to care for us when we return to Him.

TALK ABOUT IT

What did Jesus know about Peter?

When has Jesus warned you about your weakness?

How have you known Jesus' comfort when you have been weak and failed?

Read Luke 22:7–16

Why did Jesus want His disciples to celebrate Passover? Passover helped them remember that long ago God saved the Jewish people from slavery in Egypt. Something new and greater was about to happen. Jesus would take the punishment for our sin instead of a lamb. Jesus is the "Lamb of God" who takes away the sin of the world (John 1:29). God's love is so great. Through the blood of Jesus, He forgives our sin. Through Jesus' blood, we are no longer slaves to sin. Every boy, girl, mom, and dad who trusts Jesus is forgiven and will live with Him forever.

TALK ABOUT IT

What is a special meal you look forward to with people you love?

How did Jesus use this special meal to teach His disciples something important?

For those who trust in Jesus and go to heaven someday, what do you think it will be like to sit and eat with Jesus?

Read Luke 22:17–23

How was Jesus' meal different from the Passover meal? Instead of eating the Passover meal and remembering that God saved the people from slavery in Egypt, Jesus said to eat His supper and remember that He died to save us from our slavery to sin. Now, whenever we eat the Lord's Supper (Communion), we remember God's love and Jesus' great sacrifice for us. We remember Jesus' sacrifice and also look forward to His return. We will eat this supper with Him when He comes again. Jesus gave His life for the forgiveness of our sin, so we can live with Him in heaven, forever.

TALK ABOUT IT

What do we remember when we eat the Lord's Supper?

How does your church celebrate the Lord's Supper?

What is special about Jesus giving us a meal to help us remember what He has done for us?

Read Mark 14:43–52

Why did Jesus let the soldiers arrest Him? Jesus did not resist because He chose to perfectly obey His Father's will. Jesus could have called on an army of angels to save Him. But Jesus wanted to do His Father's will more than free Himself from the soldiers. One of the disciples thought he would try to help Jesus. He pulled out his sword and cut off Malchus' ear. Malchus was the servant of the high priest. Before anything worse could happen, Jesus told His disciple to put the sword away. Then Jesus went to Malchus, touched him, and healed his wound. The Lord Jesus was treated wrongly so you could be made right with God.

TALK ABOUT IT

Why did Jesus let the soldiers arrest Him?

How did Judas betray Jesus?

How would you have reacted if you were one of Jesus' disciples that night?

Read Mark 14:55–65

Why did the religious leaders want to accuse Jesus? If the religious leaders could accuse Jesus of a crime, they could have Him killed. Jesus knew He would be falsely accused. When the high priest questioned Him, Jesus said He was the Messiah, Son of Man and Son of God. The high priest tore his clothes as if he was sad. But he was actually pleased that he could now accuse Jesus of blasphemy—the most terrible crime a person could commit against God. If Jesus had not been telling the truth, He would have been guilty of blasphemy. But this was not blasphemy. The Lord Jesus truly is the Messiah!

TALK ABOUT IT

Why did the religious leaders want to accuse Jesus?

Why was it not right to accuse Jesus of blasphemy?

Why do you think Jesus, at first, remained silent, even though they were saying false things about Him?

Read Mark 15:1–15

How did Pilate respond to Jesus? Pilate tried to release Jesus. He could see that Jesus had been falsely accused by the religious leaders. Unfortunately, he also wanted to please the religious leaders and keep his job. Pilate told the people he would release Jesus and keep the prisoner, Barabbas, a convicted murderer. The people demanded that Pilate release Barabbas, instead of Jesus. Pilate and the people refused to believe in Jesus as the Messiah. The Lord Jesus was declared guilty so you could be set free from sin.

TALK ABOUT IT

What did Pilate ask Jesus? What did Pilate ask the people?

What are some differences between Barabbas and Jesus?

How are you like Pilate? How are you like Barabbas?

Read Luke 23:33–38

What happened to Jesus as he hung on the cross? Jesus suffered. His body was cut, beaten, and bruised. Jesus, the King of creation, was hung between two criminals. Just as Satan did in the wilderness, the people tempted Jesus to prove He was the Son of God. Jesus had the power to come down from the cross. He had no sins of His own. He deserved no punishment. But He took the wrath of God in our place.[3]

TALK ABOUT IT

In what ways did Jesus suffer on the cross?

How was Jesus tempted to come down from the cross?

If Jesus had the power to come down, why did He stay on the cross?

Read Luke 23:39–43

What did Jesus tell one of the men on the cross? Jesus told the one man he would be with Jesus in heaven that day. This man was repentant. That means he knew he deserved punishment. He also knew that Jesus had done nothing wrong and did not deserve to die. This man never had a chance to live another day and do anything good with his life. Yet Jesus told the man he would live with Him forever. Jesus does not wait for us to be good enough for heaven. No matter what you have done, Jesus welcomes all who repent and believe.[4]

TALK ABOUT IT

What difference is there between the two men on crosses next to Jesus?

How was the one man repentant?

What is the promise for all who repent and believe in Jesus?

Read Luke 23:44–49

What happened to the temple curtain as Jesus hung on the cross? This curtain was so tall that no one could reach the top. And it was thicker than a man's hand. The curtain that kept people from the Most Holy Place was torn in two. At the very moment Jesus died, God tore the curtain from top to bottom. Through Jesus' death, God opened the way for sinners to come to Him. Jesus died for our sins and opened the way for us to have a personal relationship with almighty God![5]

TALK ABOUT IT

What did God show us when He tore the temple curtain at the very moment Jesus died?

What did Jesus' death do for all people who repent and believe?

Would you like to be God's child? Will you repent and believe Jesus paid for your sin?

Read Matthew 28:1–6

Why were the women and guards afraid? They were afraid because an angel of the Lord came to Jesus' tomb and the earth shook violently.

The angel was brighter than lightning. He rolled back the stone that blocked the tomb. The guards fainted, but the angel told the women not to be afraid. The angel said, "I know that you seek Jesus who was crucified. He is not here, for he has risen, as he said. Come, see the place where he lay" (vv. 5–6). The tomb was empty. Jesus had risen. Jesus is God, just as He said.

TALK ABOUT IT

Why were the women and guards afraid?

What did the angel tell the women?

Who is Jesus?

Read Matthew 28:7–10

Why were the women afraid and joyful? The women were still afraid but filled with joy as they ran to tell Jesus' disciples that He was alive. Then before their very eyes, Jesus met them. Imagine how they felt to see His face, hear His voice, and touch Him. He really was alive. Jesus really is God. Now we can be sure Jesus overcame the power of death and sin. He paid the penalty for the sins of all God's children, so they will all one day rise again. God's children will live with Jesus forever, as He promised they would.

TALK ABOUT IT

What happened as the women were on their way to Jesus' disciples?

Why can we be sure Jesus overcame the power of death and sin?

How can God's children know they will one day rise again and live with Jesus forever?

Read Luke 24:1–8

What did the women believe? The women believed Jesus was dead. Instead of finding His dead body, they found an empty tomb. The angels reminded the women of the truth Jesus had told them. Jesus must die and on the third day be raised from death to life. Everything happened just as Jesus told them. Jesus meets unbelief with truth.[6]

TALK ABOUT IT

What did the women find at Jesus' tomb?

What did the angels tell the women?

What happened to Jesus?

Read Luke 24:9–11

Why did the disciples still not believe? Jesus told his disciples multiple times that He was going to die and then come to life again. But they did not yet understand what happened to Jesus' body. However, the religious leaders who hated Jesus, remembered that Jesus said He would be buried for three days and come to life again (Matt. 12:38–40). They thought the disciples might come and take Jesus' dead body out of the tomb. The religious leaders did not want anyone to believe that Jesus had the power to come to life again. Jesus was raised to life by God's power.[7]

TALK ABOUT IT

What did the disciples not yet understand about Jesus' body?

What did the religious leaders think would happen to Jesus' body?

What really happened to Jesus' body?

Read Luke 24:13–24

Why were Cleopas and his friend so sad? Jesus knew these friends were sad because they were confused. Jesus asked good questions to help them know why they were confused. They believed Jesus had power from God to rescue Israel from the cruel Roman rulers. Why hadn't Jesus used His power to kill these enemies? Instead, the enemies killed Him. On the third day when Jesus said He would rise, why had no one seen Him? Had they believed a fairy tale? They were confused because they did not know the truth. We will always be confused until Jesus leads us to the truth.[8]

TALK ABOUT IT

Why were Cleopas and his friend so sad?

What were some of the questions they had about Jesus?

What are questions you still have about Jesus?

Read Luke 24:25–27

Why did Jesus call these friends foolish? The friends knew the Bible, so they were foolish not to know the truth about Jesus. The Bible, from beginning to end, tells us about Jesus. Jesus had to suffer and die to rescue us from our sin. Sin hurts us and everyone. Most of all, sin is against God. We cannot fix the big problem of sin ourselves. God loves us so much! He sent Jesus to rescue us from sin and give us hearts to believe in Jesus. God gives us the Bible to tell us the truth about Jesus.

TALK ABOUT IT

What truth about Jesus did Cleopas and his friend not know?

Why does the Bible tell us about Jesus' rescue?

What truth about Jesus does the Bible help you understand?

Read Luke 24:30–32

What does it mean that their "hearts were burning"? It means their sadness turned to joy. The Bible cleared away their confusion about Jesus. True joy comes as we know the truth about Jesus—who He is and why He suffered. The Bible gives us evidence to believe Jesus is alive. God let them see that it was Jesus talking to them. They were happier than ever before. Now they knew—Jesus was alive! Jesus rose again, just as He said He would. Jesus truly is the Messiah King. Jesus is alive and fills our hearts with joy![9]

TALK ABOUT IT

How did these friends respond when they knew the Bible truth about Jesus?

According to Luke 24, what would you say is the main point of the whole Bible?

Talk about a time when God helped you understand the truth about Jesus.

Read Matthew 28:16–20

Why did the disciples go to Galilee? They went to Galilee because Jesus told them to meet Him there. Before Jesus went back to heaven, He told His disciples to continue His work. Jesus told them to go and tell other people in the world about Jesus. Then more people would love Jesus and obey His commands. Jesus promised to be with them always. He would send the Holy Spirit to give faith to people who hear His disciples teach about Jesus. Until Jesus comes again, His disciples love to tell people the wonderful news of His life, death, and resurrection.

TALK ABOUT IT

What did the disciples do when they saw Jesus?

What did Jesus promise His disciples?

What did Jesus tell His disciples to do?

Prayer

Jesus, we worship You as our risen King! You died, and You rose again! We want to be Your disciples, and we want to help others become Your disciples. We praise You that You have all authority in heaven and on earth. And we thank You for the promise that You will be with us always, to the end of the age.

ACTS

Introduction

The book of Acts is the sequel to the gospel of Luke (both books written by the same man—Luke). It's the continuing story of what happens after Jesus rose from the dead and ascended to heaven.

ICEBREAKER: Have you ever had to wait for something that was promised to you? What was it?

Read Acts 1:3–5

Why did Jesus tell His friends to wait in Jerusalem? They needed to wait for the gift God had promised them—the Holy Spirit. Jesus had taught them about the Holy Spirit (John 15:26–27). After Jesus returned to heaven, they would be baptized with the Holy Spirit. Through the Holy Spirit, Jesus would come to live in them. The Holy Spirit would give them new desires to love and please God. He gives us new minds to think His way. God gives the gift of the Holy Spirit to all who trust in Jesus.[10]

TALK ABOUT IT

Why did Jesus tell his disciples to wait in Jerusalem?

What changes happen in our hearts when God gives us a new heart?

If you have put your trust in Jesus, how has the Holy Spirit helped you want to love God?

Read Acts 1:8–11

What did Jesus promise His friends? Jesus promised them the gift of the Holy Spirit. Jesus had told His friends to go into the whole world and tell people about Him (Matt. 28:19–20). But by themselves, they could never convince anyone to believe. Only God can change a person's mind and heart. Without the Holy Spirit, no one can believe the truth about Jesus. The Holy Spirit would give Jesus' friends the power to tell people everywhere about Him. The Holy Spirit gives us power to tell people the truth about Jesus.

TALK ABOUT IT

Why would the disciples not be able to do what Jesus told them to do?

What does the Holy Spirit do that we cannot?

When have you known the Holy Spirit's power to do what God wants?

Read Acts 2:1–6

Where were Jesus' friends on the day of Pentecost? Jesus' friends were in Jerusalem, waiting for the gift Jesus had promised. Suddenly, a loud sound like strong wind from heaven filled their house. Something like flames of fire rested on each of Jesus' friends. God was giving them the Holy Spirit! Filled with the Spirit, Jesus' friends began to speak languages they did not know. But Jews from every nation and language were in Jerusalem. Imagine their surprise when they heard Jesus' friends praising God in their own languages! God planned for people from all languages to know the truth about Jesus.

TALK ABOUT IT

What did Jesus' friends hear and see when they were together in Jerusalem?

Who understood the different languages that Jesus' friends spoke?

What did God want people from all languages to know?

Read Acts 2:36–40

How did the people respond to Peter? The Holy Spirit made them sad about their sin. They were "cut to the heart" and asked, "what shall we do?" (v. 37). Peter told them to repent. To repent means we turn away from our sin and trust in Jesus. When we trust in Jesus, we believe He died to forgive our sin. Peter promised God would forgive them. God would save them from His judgment and give the Holy Spirit to live in them. What should we do? Repent! Turn from sin and trust in Jesus. To trust in Jesus is to be forgiven, saved, and given the Holy Spirit.

TALK ABOUT IT

What did the Holy Spirit do?

What does it mean to repent?

What does God do for those who trust in Jesus?

Read Acts 5:1–11

What happened to Ananias and Sapphira? They pretended to give all their money to the church. Satan tempted them to want people to notice and praise them. They cared more about looking good than having hearts right with God. God helped Peter know that they had lied to the Holy Spirit. God hates sin. He sees our hearts and knows we need holiness to live together. Satan tries to use our sin to stop the spread of God's truth. God's quick judgment shows how much He wants our hearts to be right. God is holy and calls His children to be holy.

TALK ABOUT IT

What did Ananias and Saphira do? Why was this wrong?

Who influenced them to do this?

What lesson did the church learn from this?

Read Acts 5:17–20, 27–33, 40–42

What happened after Ananias and Sapphira died? Those who did not believe in Jesus feared God's judgment. But those who believed had a holy fear of God. They wanted to respect and obey God. Satan tried to stop the spread of God's truth. Instead, more and more people believed in Jesus. As the church grew, the Jewish leaders grew more jealous. They angrily jailed and beat the apostles but later freed them. The apostles rejoiced because they were counted worthy to suffer for Jesus. God's children can trust His plan to use every problem for their good and His glory.

TALK ABOUT IT

Who opposed the apostles? Why?

What happened to the church when Satan tried to stop the spread of God's truth?

How were the apostles able to rejoice in their time of trouble?

Read Acts 6:8–15; 7:51–53

How did the Jewish leaders react to Stephen? They rejected Stephen because he was full of God's grace and power. They lied and said Stephen spoke against Moses and God. They grabbed Stephen and took him to the Jewish leaders for a trial. They charged Stephen with speaking against the law and the temple. But he had simply preached the truth. Stephen said Jesus fulfilled the law through His sinless life. Jesus is the true temple. God confirmed Stephen and his message. Everyone could see that Stephen's face looked like the face of an angel. When people reject the truth God confirms His faithful witnesses.

TALK ABOUT IT

What did the Jewish leaders do to Stephen?

How did Stephen defend himself?

Have you ever been rejected when you talked with friends about Jesus?

Read Acts 7:54–60

What happened when Stephen said the Jewish leaders had killed Jesus? They angrily dragged him out of the city and threw stones at him. But God did not abandon Stephen. Full of the Holy Spirit, Stephen looked up and saw Jesus standing at the right hand of God. Stephen died trusting God would use his faithful witness. Yet who could imagine how God would use Stephen's death for good? Through Stephen's final prayer, God changed the heart of Saul—Stephen's greatest enemy—into the apostle Paul. God does more than we can imagine with our lives for His good purposes.

TALK ABOUT IT

How did God help Stephen?

As Stephen was dying, what did he say that was similar to something Jesus said when He was on the cross? See Luke 23:34.

How might God use you to change the heart of those who hear?

Read Acts 8:1–8

What happened after Stephen was killed? Saul put many of Jesus' followers in prison. Most believers ran from Jerusalem to escape. They fled to Judea and Samaria—places Jews never wanted to go. But God had a plan. As a farmer scatters seed to produce a crop, God scattered believers so many would hear the truth about Jesus. The Samaritans had God's Word. But they had mixed God's truth with lies. The Holy Spirit worked powerfully as Philip preached the good news of Jesus. Just as Jesus had promised (Acts 1:8), many people believed. God uses opposition to carry out His plans.

TALK ABOUT IT

What was Saul doing?

How did persecution help to spread the good news?

What was the response to Philip's ministry?

Read Acts 9:1–8, 17–19

What happened to Saul? Saul left Jerusalem to arrest believers in Jesus in Damascus. On the road to Damascus, a bright light flashed around Saul. He fell down, blinded by the light. A voice asked, "Saul, Saul, why are you persecuting me?" Jesus was speaking. When Saul hurt Christians, he hurt Jesus. Jesus is Lord. When Jesus told Saul to go into Damascus and wait, Saul obeyed. Jesus sent Ananias to Saul. Saul turned from his sin and trusted in Jesus. Now Saul could see! Jesus calls all people everywhere to turn from sin and trust Him.

TALK ABOUT IT

In your own words, tell what happened to Saul.

Why do you think Jesus loved a man who had hurt so many people?

Have you wondered if Jesus would ever love you? Will you turn from sin and trust Jesus now?

Prayer

Father God, we praise You for sending the gift of the Holy Spirit. You are faithful to keep Your promises! Thank You for giving us boldness through Your Spirit to share Your truth with others. May Your Spirit convict us of our sin and help us to trust in You with all that You call us to do.

ROMANS

Introduction

After the Gospels and Acts, we come to the letters of the New Testament. From the letter to the Romans all the way to the letter to Titus—these letters were written by the apostle Paul (Saul). Paul wrote letters to churches in various cities, and he wrote letters to individuals. In Paul's letter to the Romans, he shares the gospel about Jesus in great detail and with much depth.

ICEBREAKER: Talk about a time when you worked really hard to earn something.

Read Romans 1:1–17

What did Paul mean by saying he was an apostle? An apostle is a special teacher called by God to tell people about Jesus. The twelve disciples of Jesus were apostles. This was a big change for Paul who had been known and feared for his hatred of Jesus and Jesus' followers. Paul was also known as Saul. Saul belonged to the religious group called the Pharisees. Before he believed in Jesus as his Savior, Saul saw Jesus as an enemy of God's people. But Jesus came to Saul in a special way, changed his heart, and gave him faith to believe that Jesus was not an enemy. Jesus is the Messiah who came to save God's people. The gospel is the good news about Jesus. How He lived, died, and was resurrected for the forgiveness of our sins. To believe in Jesus means to believe who He is and that He makes us right with God. To be right with God is to be counted righteous by faith in Jesus. No one is righteous except by believing in Jesus.

TALK ABOUT IT

Who wrote this letter? And to whom did he write it?

What does it mean that Paul was an apostle?

In your own words, describe Paul's purpose in writing this letter.

Read Romans 1:18–21

Why do some people not worship God? They do not worship God because they do not want to. No one can ever say God is not real. God shows Himself to us every day. Every time we see the beauty of the sky, stars, and moon, we know God is real. When we hear the birds or feel a gentle breeze or smell the sweetness of a flower, we know He is our powerful Creator. We know the stars and flowers did not create themselves. Someone loving and powerful made them and that is God. We do not look at a painting and say the picture painted itself. We know an artist painted it. When we look at creation, we know God made it. There is no excuse for not believing in God. God, our Creator, is worthy of all our love and worship.

TALK ABOUT IT

What excuse can people give for not believing in God?

How does God let us know He is real?

How will you thank God and worship Him for what He has made?

Read Romans 1:22–32

What do people worship when they don't worship God? Everyone worships something. Until we really love God, we worship things called idols. Some idols are statues made of wood, but idols can also be things we put before God. Our idols are things we buy or things we do to make ourselves happy. There's nothing wrong with new clothes. But if new clothes are the best way to make me happy, they have become my idol. Our idols will only make us happy for a while, but God gives true happiness forever. What does God give to people who do not worship Him? God lets them worship what they want to worship. That means if someone wants to worship themselves by disobeying their parents or lying or doing evil things, God will let them feel the pain of living that way. When people refuse God's love they see His wrath. God's wrath is His judgment on whatever is working against Him. Everyone who works against God deserves His judgment for their sin. The Bible tells us something else about God's wrath. When Jesus hung on the cross, He took the full wrath of God for our sin. Now, all who turn from their sin to believe in Jesus are given God's forgiveness instead of wrath (1 Peter 2:24.)

TALK ABOUT IT

What do people worship other than God?

What is God's wrath?

Consider what idols are in your heart that you need to repent of.

Read Romans 2:1–4

How do we know God's judgment is right? We know God's judgment is right because of who God is. He is the only one who can judge fairly. God is righteous and holy, so all His decisions are righteous and holy. God is impartial; He never shows favoritism. Each person, no matter who they are, will receive a right and fair judgment by God. We do not judge fairly, and we often show favoritism to ourselves. It is easy for us to see when someone else does wrong, but it's hard to admit when we do what is wrong. We are quick to judge others and slow to judge ourselves. We might even think God will judge everyone else but not us.

TALK ABOUT IT

Who is the only one fair in all His judgments?

What does it mean that God is impartial?

When has it been hard for you to admit you were wrong?

Read Romans 2:5–16

How will we be judged by God? God will judge each person fairly. Each person will stand before God, and He will say we are guilty or not guilty for the way we lived our life. We learn about the way God wants us to live from the Bible. But what about the people who have not grown up reading the Bible or going to church? How will God judge them? God created each person with a built-in compass called a conscience. Just like a compass shows which way to go on a trail, our inner compass, or conscience, tells us when we are doing what is right or wrong. No one will be able say to God they did not know there was a right and wrong way to live. Even though each person knows what is right, no one does what is right all the time. All people have done something wrong even when they knew what was right.

TALK ABOUT IT

How will each person be judged by God?

How does a person know what is right and wrong?

When have you known something was wrong and did it anyway?

Read Romans 2:17–29

How can we be saved from God's judgment? Can we be saved from judgment if we do the right things—joining the church, helping other people, and obeying our parents—all the time? It is good to do what is right, but no one does what is right all the time. If we live in a

Christian family, will God forget about the judgment we deserve? The Jewish people in the church in Rome said God would not judge them because they were special to God and He gave them His law and circumcision. But it is what God sees in each person's heart that matters most. God saw their hearts were sinful. How then can anyone be saved from God's wrath and eternal punishment in hell? In God's love and mercy, He sent Jesus to live a perfect and righteous life for us. God sent Jesus to die for us. On the cross, Jesus took the wrath and punishment for sin that we deserve. Through faith in Jesus, God gives us a new heart and the righteousness of Jesus. Jesus Christ changes our hearts and saves us from God's judgment.

TALK ABOUT IT

What good things do people think will save them from God's judgment?

Why do these good things not save us from God's judgment?

What is the only way to be saved from God's judgment?

Read Romans 4:1–12

Who was Abraham? Abraham was a good man who loved God. But before Abraham loved God or ever did anything good, God loved him. In Genesis 15, God told Abraham that even though he did not have any children, he would have a big family and then a son who would bless the whole world. Abraham's family would be large. And God planned for one of Abraham's descendants to save us from our sins. Years later, just as God planned, Jesus was born through the family line of Abraham. Abraham believed the promises of God about Jesus (John 8:56.) Abraham was justified, meaning he was given Jesus' righteousness. He was justified not because he was good but because he had faith in God's promises. We are God's children by faith in Jesus not our good works.

TALK ABOUT IT

What promise about Jesus did God give Abraham?

What is the connection between earning and boasting? Explain how God's plan of salvation is different than this.

How does it make you feel that eternal salvation is offered to you freely, not by works but by trusting in Jesus?

Read Romans 5:1–11

What does God say about those who have faith in Jesus? God says they are justified. To be justified means that God will never look at you and say "guilty" again. Now God, the judge of the universe, says of us who have faith in Jesus, "You are My child." How do we know our faith in Jesus is real? We know our faith is real when our suffering makes us stronger and gives us hope. Suffering is normal for God's children and makes them more like Jesus. Our troubles are like climbing a steep hill with the wind in our face. But God comes to take our hand, protect us, and help us walk uprightly.

TALK ABOUT IT

What does it mean to be justified?

What does suffering do to our faith in Jesus?

When has God made your faith stronger through suffering?

Read Romans 5:12–19

What did Adam bring into the world? Adam brought sin into the world. Through sin came death. God created Adam in His image. There was no pain or death. Then Adam and Eve listened to Satan's lies and sinned. They lost their perfect relationship with God. Like a beautiful picture dropped in mud, they could no longer show God's image clearly. Because God made Adam the father of all people, we are all born into Adam's family, with no desire or ability to obey God. Now we are all born like the muddy picture. We experience hardship, sickness, and the punishment for sin, which is death. Jesus Christ brought something different into the world than Adam did. Jesus brought a gift of God's grace that changed everything. Jesus brings God's grace to God's children so they can show His image. Jesus can wash us clean no matter how muddy our life is. Adam's sin brought us condemnation and death. Jesus brings justification and life to the full! His death and righteous life wash away the sins of all who believe in Him.

TALK ABOUT IT

What did Adam bring into the world?

What did Jesus bring to God's children?

What changes does God's grace make for those who believe in Jesus?

Read Romans 6:1–11

If God always forgives His children, why does it matter if we sin? It matters because God's children are united to Jesus. To be united to Jesus means God takes us out of the family of Adam and puts us in His family with Jesus (Rom. 5:12–17). In the family of Adam, we were slaves to sin. Sin owned us and told us what to do. In God's family, Jesus set us free from slavery to sin. We no longer have to sin because Jesus gives us His power to obey God. It is wrong to think that because God forgives us, we can keep sinning. God's children are most happy when they think, speak, and act like Jesus.

TALK ABOUT IT

Why does it matter if we sin?

What does it mean to be united to Jesus?

What difference should verse 11 make in the lives of Christians? How can we put this into practice?

Read Romans 6:15–23

How are we either a slave to sin or a slave to obedience? No one is their own master, not presidents, parents, or principals. Without faith in Jesus, all people are slaves to sin. They are not free to love and serve God as long as they do what sin tells them to. Why would we want to have a cruel master like sin who pays us with death? God is the only good master. He frees us to love and serve Him. He gives us life in His family with Jesus forever. God's children are most happy when they are living for God and serving Him.

TALK ABOUT IT

Why are people without faith in Jesus slaves to sin?

Why is God the only good master?

When have you been happy serving God?

Read Romans 8:1–15

Why is there no condemnation for those in Christ Jesus? There is no condemnation for us because on the cross, God condemned our sin fully in Jesus. Everything Jesus did in His life and His death counts for God's children. God promises that there is no condemnation now or forever for any of His children.

What is the difference between living by the flesh and living by the Spirit? The flesh is not just our body. It is everything a person is before he or she believes in Jesus. Those who live by the flesh are controlled by whatever sinful thing they want. They don't want what God wants, so they cannot do or say what pleases God. When we believe in Jesus it is as if God puts us in a whole new world—the world of His Spirit. Everyone who believes in Jesus has His Spirit. Those who live by the Spirit want what God wants. They want to please God with what they think, say, and do.

TALK ABOUT IT

Why is there no condemnation for God's children?

What does it mean to live by the flesh?

What does it mean to live by the Spirit?

Read Romans 8:16–27

What is the glory Jesus shares with us? The glory of Jesus is all He has and is. Jesus shares all He is and has with God's children. The son of a wealthy father may inherit lots of money and honor from his father. But no earthly father has riches or honor like our heavenly Father. Jesus, as God's Son, inherits God's riches and honor. And Jesus shares all His riches and honor with us. On earth we share Jesus' suffering—but only for a short time. In heaven we will share a new glorified body like His. Best of all, we will share the wonder of being with God.

TALK ABOUT IT

What is the glory of Jesus?

What does Jesus share with God's children?

What are you most excited about seeing in heaven?

Read Romans 8:28–30

What does God do for those who love Him? God promises to make everything that happens in the lives of His children work toward a happiness that never ends. Whatever makes you feel happy—a roller coaster ride, swimming, playing the piano—God's happiness gives your heart much more joy. His happiness is yours as you are most like Jesus. Whatever comes into our lives, God has put it there to make us like Jesus. God uses good things and hard things to make us more like Jesus. When God's answer is no to things we ask for, we can remember God gives us nothing that takes away from our eternal happiness.

TALK ABOUT IT

What does God promise to give His children?

When are God's children most happy?

When has God used something hard to make you more like Jesus?

Read Romans 8:31–39

How do we know God loves us? We know of God's love because He gave up His *Son* for *us*! If He did this, what will He not do for us? Nothing! Even the best gift a child could receive from his parent does not compare to God's gift of Jesus to His children. You can know God is keeping His promise to work everything in your life for good because He has already given Jesus for you. And whatever hard thing happens, not one thing can ever separate God's child from His love for them in Jesus.

TALK ABOUT IT

How do you know God loves you?

What are some hard things in life that could threaten to separate us from the love of God?

How does it encourage you to know that Christians are "more than conquerors" (v. 37)?

Read Romans 9:1–18

Why was Paul so sad? Paul was sad because His people, the Israelites, did not know God. God showed the Israelites His divine glory. He gave them special covenant promises and His Word. Best of all, God promised to send the Messiah to them. But they did not believe Jesus was the Messiah. Did God's promises to the people of Israel fail? No, God is faithful to His promises. God will save all the people of Israel, who are His true children, from His judgment and wrath. But no one is automatically God's child. Then and now, only those who believe in the Savior God promised to send are God's children. To show that salvation is not by anything we do but only because of His mercy, God chose Jacob to love Him. God has the right to show mercy to some and allow others to continue in unbelief. Although we may have questions about why some people do not believe, we can trust God always.

TALK ABOUT IT

Why was Paul sad?

What does God's sovereign choice teach us about salvation and about God?

What questions do you have about God's plans?

Read Romans 12:1–2

What is the best way for God's children to live? God's children know that the best way to live is to give their whole life to God. Because of

God's mercy to us, He is worthy of all our thoughts, time, and energy. We often think we will be happiest when we live to please ourselves. But we are most happy when we live and think in a way that pleases God. How do we learn to think in a way that pleases God? God's Word changes our way of thinking, so we learn how good God's will is, even when it is hard. This gives the most joy to our hearts.

TALK ABOUT IT

Why is God worthy of all our thoughts, time, and energy?

How do we learn to think in a way that pleases God?

What plan do you have for reading God's Word?

Read Romans 12:3–8

How do God's children serve each other? God gives gifts to each of His children, so we can serve each other. The gifts are from God, so we cannot be proud of our gifts or jealous of another's gift. Our gifts are for the good of others. God gives so many powerful gifts! Teaching, encouraging, leading, giving, and showing mercy are just a few. When we use our gifts, we help other people in the church grow to be like Jesus. When we use our gifts generously and cheerfully, we grow to love each other too.

TALK ABOUT IT

How do God's children serve each other?

What happens when we use our gifts to help people?

When has someone used their gifts to help you grow more like Jesus?

Read Romans 12:9–21

How are God's children to love others? We make up our mind to hate what is evil and love what is good. We honor others more than we honor ourselves. We share with God's children who are in need. We bless those who hate God's children and do not hate them back. We love others who are not as smart or have less money or do not have friends. We do not return evil for evil. God tells us that to love others is not easy! What help do we have? God gives His children power to love others. And God says He will judge rightly.

TALK ABOUT IT

How are God's children to love others?

What help does God give us to love others even when it is hard?

When has God helped you love someone when it was hard?

Read Romans 13:1–7

What are governing authorities? Parents, teachers, church leaders, and government officials are some of the people who have authority over us. God places authorities over us for our good. We may not like to do homework, but when our teacher assigns it, we owe the homework to our teacher. And we may not want to do chores, but when our parents tell us, we owe obedience to our parents. Not everyone is in authority over us, but God says to give to everyone what you owe them. If respect, then respect; if honor, then honor.

TALK ABOUT IT

Who are the governing authorities in your life?

What do you owe your authorities?

When has your mom or dad given you a chore you didn't want to do? Or when has a teacher given you an assignment you didn't want to do? How did you react?

Read Romans 14:1–12

Why are God's children supposed to accept each other? The reason God's children accept each other is that they both belong to God. It is not up to us to decide to reject each other. We are to love each other. If God's Word has not told us what to do, then our choices may differ from one another. If God's Word has not told us which songs to sing, we cannot argue with other children of God if they sing different songs. When God's Word does not tell us which school to attend, we cannot quarrel with other children of God when they or their parents make a different choice of school.

TALK ABOUT IT

For the Christians in Rome, what were some of the disagreements they had among one another?

Why are God's children to accept each other?

When is it not right to argue about choices with other children of God?

Read Romans 14:13–23

What does it mean to cause someone to stumble? To stumble means to fall. When someone puts a brick on a path, it could cause another person to fall. People can cause someone to stumble in a spiritual way too. If I demand my own way more than helping my friend do what they believe is right, this may cause them to stumble and sin. When we stick out our foot, we can cause someone to fall and get hurt. When we stick to demanding our right to do something, we can cause someone to fall into sin. This is not acting in love. God wants us to love other children of God.

TALK ABOUT IT

What does it mean to stumble in a spiritual way?

Why is it loving to want another child of God to do what they believe is right?

When have you acted more on your rights than out of love?

Prayer

God, we praise You for Your sovereign power to change even the hardest hearts. Thank You for the amazing conversion of Paul who became an apostle for You. We praise You for the free gift of salvation through faith in Christ. There is nothing that we can do to earn favor with You, it is only through faith in the blood of Jesus. Help us to gladly receive the gift of salvation through Christ.

1 & 2 CORINTHIANS

Introduction

Paul wrote these letters to the Christians in the city of Corinth. Corinth was a city, and a church, with many problems. Paul wrote to the believers in Corinth because he wanted them to become more like Jesus and more unified in their worship of Jesus.

1 Corinthians

ICEBREAKER: What makes it hard to get along with others sometimes?

Read 1 Corinthians 1:11–31

Why don't Christians always get along? Paul heard from Chloe that the Christians in the city of Corinth were not getting along with each other. So Paul wrote a letter to the church in that city to help them with their many problems. In this first chapter, Paul tells them to be unified, not divided. There are many different leaders and teachers among God's people. But there's only one Savior, our Lord Jesus Christ. When we keep our focus on Jesus and the good news of His salvation, that will bring us closer together. In the world's thinking, the good news of Jesus dying on a cross doesn't make sense. But God's way of doing things is so different, and better, than the ways of the world.

TALK ABOUT IT

What were some of the differences that were dividing the believers in Corinth?

What are some differences among believers today?

How can believers be united, rather than divided?

Read 1 Corinthians 15:1–17

Why is the resurrection of Jesus so important? In his letter to the church in Corinth, Paul wrote a lot about how important it is that Jesus not only died on the cross but also rose again on the third day. This is what the Old Testament said would happen. And many people saw Jesus alive again after He had died on the cross. Paul teaches us that the good news about Jesus wouldn't really be true if Jesus was still in the tomb. Our faith in Jesus wouldn't really mean anything if Jesus didn't rise from the dead.

TALK ABOUT IT

In Paul's teaching in 1 Corinthians 15, what does he say is so important?

If Jesus didn't rise from the dead, what would that mean for us?

What would you say to a friend who doubts that Jesus really rose from the dead?

Prayer

Lord Jesus, thank You that You are the supreme leader of the church. Forgive us when we fight and quarrel with others instead of looking to You. Help us to be unified with other believers, lifting our eyes off ourselves and onto You. Help us to be peacemakers with others for our good and Your glory. Jesus, we look to You as our risen Savior. We know that You died, and that You also walked out of the grave on the third day. You are alive! We can talk to You today, and always.

2 Corinthians

ICEBREAKER: When have you given something away and it made you happy? Have you ever had to give something away that made you sad?

Read 2 Corinthians 8:1–9

What does it mean to be generous? God wants His children to be generous, which means He wants us to give freely to others from the things He has given to us. In 2 Corinthians 8–9, Paul writes to the church in Corinth about giving to a collection that will help needy believers in Jerusalem (see 1 Cor. 16:1–4). To encourage the church in Corinth, Paul tells them about the radical generosity of the believers in Macedonia. They were so eager to give, they gave more than they could afford to give! In this passage, Paul also writes about the generosity of our Lord Jesus Christ. Jesus set aside the riches of His place in heaven in order to live in this sinful world and to die on the cross. He did this to save poor sinners like us and to give us the rich inheritance of eternal life!

TALK ABOUT IT

What does it mean to be generous?

Why were the Macedonians so generous? What motivated them?

How do we benefit from the generosity of our Lord Jesus Christ?

Read 2 Corinthians 9:6–15

How can we give cheerfully? If your mom or dad tells you to give a piece of your candy to your brother or sister, that may be difficult to do. You might not want to give away something that's yours, especially if it's something you really like. In these verses of God's Word, we read that "God loves a cheerful giver" (v. 7). God has been generous to us, and He loves it when we give generously, and joyfully, to others. In Acts 20:35, Paul quotes the words of Jesus, who said, "It is more blessed to give than to receive." When God changes our heart, He helps us to experience the excitement of giving. Then we realize it's actually more fun to give things away to bless others, than it is to get more and more stuff for ourselves.

TALK ABOUT IT

When have you been required to give something away that you didn't want to?

How has God been generous to you?

When have you felt the joy of giving something away to bless someone else?

Prayer

Father God, thank You for the reminder that You love a cheerful giver! Thank You for the example of the Macedonians giving so generously to other believers in need. Help us to hold our possessions loosely, to know that it is more blessed to give than to receive. Encourage us to be generous with all that You've entrusted to us.

GALATIANS

Introduction

Galatians is a letter Paul wrote to the churches in the region of Galatia. These churches were in danger of losing the heart of the gospel because false teachers were trying to lead them astray. Paul wrote this letter to warn them and protect them. He reminded them of the wonderful truth of the gospel—that we're not saved by doing but by trusting.

ICEBREAKER: Have you ever had a disagreement with a friend? What was it about?

Read Galatians 2:11–21

Why did Paul oppose Peter? Paul was very serious about helping the early church understand that salvation is through faith alone, and not by working to keep the Jewish laws. Peter understood this too. Peter knew that it was okay to eat with Gentiles, even though that meant breaking Jewish food laws. But when certain men came to town, Peter felt pressured to go back to the Jewish customs. This may not seem like a big deal. But it gave the impression that keeping the Jewish food laws (and other laws, like circumcision) was necessary for salvation. So Paul confronted Peter because Peter's behavior "was not in step with the truth of the gospel" (v. 14).

TALK ABOUT IT

Why did Paul oppose Peter?

In what way were Peter and others acting hypocritically?

What does it mean to be justified (counted righteous) through faith in Jesus and not by works of the law?

Read Galatians 5:16–23

What is the battle between the flesh and the Spirit? Our flesh (or sinful nature) is a result of Adam and Eve disobeying God in the garden of Eden. Ever since then, each person (except Jesus) has been deeply influenced by these sinful desires that are with us from the very start of our lives. But those who put their trust in Jesus and repent of their sins receive the Holy Spirit as our new helper and guide. So from the time a person becomes a Christian, they have this battle going on between the old fleshly desires and the new influence of the Holy Spirit. In these verses, Paul tells us to walk by the Spirit and to fight against the destructive behaviors and attitudes of the flesh.

TALK ABOUT IT

What is the battle between the flesh and the Spirit?

Name one or two works of the flesh you have experienced in your life.

Name some fruit of the Spirit you have experienced and want to experience more.

Prayer

Heavenly Father, we praise You for Your patience with us. Thank You that even when we mess up, You are gracious to forgive us. Thank You for friends who confront us when we're acting foolish, like Paul did to Peter. Help us to walk by the Spirit, and to fight against the desires of the flesh. We pray for the Spirit to produce in us love, joy, peace, patience, kindness, goodness, faithfulness, gentleness, and self-control.

EPHESIANS

Introduction

Paul wrote this letter to the church in the city of Ephesus. Paul was in jail in Rome when he wrote this letter (3:1; 4:1; 6:20). He wanted to encourage the believers in Ephesus with great truths about God, the good news of Jesus Christ, and how we are to live as Christians. He also wanted to let them know how he was doing (6:21–22). And Paul writes out his prayers for them (1:15–23; 3:14–21).

ICEBREAKER: **What is the best gift you ever received? Why?**

Read Ephesians 1:1–14

What did Paul want the people to know about God? Paul wanted the people in Ephesus to know that God blesses those who believe in Jesus. Through Jesus, we become a child in God's family. God does not choose to adopt us because we are good enough but because He wants our life to glorify him. To glorify God means your life shows God's image. Like a mirror shows your image, God's children show God's image. It is not about becoming perfect enough to show God's image but about how God shows His image through imperfect people.

TALK ABOUT IT

What does it mean to be adopted?

What is God's great purpose in adopting us (see vv. 6, 12, and 4).

How can we glorify God?

Read Ephesians 1:1–14 (again)

What is redemption? When Jesus came to earth as a man, He paid the penalty for sin so all who believe in Him can be saved. He provided our redemption. Redemption means Jesus paid for our salvation with His blood. Believers in Jesus are redeemed or set free from the penalty of sin and slavery to sin. To be redeemed by Jesus is to be rich because God gives the greatest gifts ever. God gives the Holy Spirit to live in His children. The Holy Spirit gives new power to live a holy life. The Holy Spirit lets God's child know they belong to God forever. You might mark your name on a school folder with permanent ink so it never gets lost. God "marks" His children with the Holy Spirit to show they belong to Him forever.

TALK ABOUT IT

What does redemption mean?

What does God "mark" His children with so they are His forever?

How powerful is God? What are some things Paul says in these verses about God's power?

Read Ephesians 1:15–23

What was Paul's prayer? Paul prayed that believers would know about the riches and power they have because of Jesus. It is sad when someone does not know they are rich and lives like they are poor. God's children need to know of the great treasure He has for them. God's Word and His Holy Spirit are treasures for us. God's treasures work in our hearts, so we show His image wherever we go and bring glory to Him in whatever we do.

TALK ABOUT IT

Why was Paul thankful?

What does Paul want the Ephesians (and us) to know (see vv. 18–19)?

For those who know these things, how does it change the way we live?

Read Ephesians 2:1–10

What does it mean when it says, "you were dead" (v. 1)? It means that even though a person's body is alive, their spirit is dead toward God. You may think you have never sinned, but no one loves God with all their heart. And no one loves their parents or obeys them all the time. We are all guilty of sin. This bad news gets worse. Unbelievers are dead and deserve God's wrath. God's anger is not like ours. As the King of the universe, it is right for God to judge sin. How is it possible for someone to be "made alive" (v. 5)? It is not possible for human beings to do this. But God's love for us is so great that He sent Jesus to live on earth. Jesus took the punishment for sin that we deserve, when He died on the cross. A person who believes in Jesus is no longer dead. Jesus gives life to our spirit and makes our heart alive to God. Even though we were dead and deserved God's wrath, He gives us life with Him forever.

TALK ABOUT IT

What does it mean that our heart is dead?

How is it possible for someone to be "made alive"?

What is God's grace?

Read Ephesians 2:1–10 (again)

Why are we given life? We are not given life because of good things we do. Dead people are not able to do good things. We are given life because of God's grace. Grace is God's kindness to those who do not deserve it. God's grace means He reaches our spirit with His power to make us alive even though we are dead in sin. His grace gives us faith to believe in Jesus. When we believe in Jesus and are alive, we become useful to God like a fan is useful after it is plugged in to electricity. When we are "plugged in" to God, we are ready to do the special work He has for us. God has special work for each of us to do during the days of our life on earth. God's special work for you will glorify Him.

TALK ABOUT IT

If we earned salvation by doing good things, what would that lead to (see vv. 8–9)?

Are good works still important?

What are some good works God has prepared for you to do?

Read Ephesians 3

What mystery did God show Paul? God showed Paul the mystery that Jews and Gentiles who believe in Jesus are brought together to make one new group called the church. A mystery is something that was hidden and is now made known. It was not fully known that God loved the Gentiles and planned to include them in His family. What did Paul pray for his friends? He prayed for them to understand how special it is to be in God's family, the church. God gives great strength to people who trust in Jesus. Why did Paul pray for his friends? Paul knew they would think more about their weaknesses and why they cannot do the things God wants them to do. But God's power in us is so strong that He can do more than we can imagine. When God lets you know He has something for you to do, even if you feel afraid, He will give the strength you need.

TALK ABOUT IT

What mystery did God show Paul?

How does God's love fill our hearts?

Think about Paul's prayers in Ephesians 1 and Ephesians 3. How can these prayers teach you how to pray?

Read Ephesians 4:1–16

What gifts did Jesus give us? Jesus' gifts to us are the people in the church who help us grow up in our love for God. Jesus gives you people like pastors, Sunday school teachers, and parents to help you learn about Jesus' love for you. Why did Jesus give us these gifts? God wants us to listen to adults who love and follow Jesus, so we will grow up and believe the truth of God's Word. Did you know your love for God needs to grow? If we do not grow up in our love for God, we stay spiritual babies. Little babies put everything in their mouths and cannot tell the difference between what will help them and what will hurt them. Spiritual babies listen to what anyone says, even if it is false and will hurt them. With the truth of His Word in your heart, you will become strong in your love for God. When you are strong in your love for God, you will be strong in your love for others.

TALK ABOUT IT

What does it mean to be humble?

Name some people in your life, and in your church, who are God's gifts to you.

How can you know if you are a spiritual baby or growing up in your love for God?

Read Ephesians 4:17–32

How do God's children grow up? God's children grow up as they put away their old way of life and put on the new way of life. When someone's body grows up, they put away the old clothes that no longer fit and put on new clothes that do fit. God wants all His children to grow up and live more like Jesus. That means they have to put away the things they used to do. To put away our old way of life means to put away sinful living and put on Christlike living. Once we believe Jesus is God's Son and our Savior, we live in a new way.

TALK ABOUT IT

What new way of thinking does God want you to have?

What old way of life do you need to put away?

What new way of life do you need to put on?

Read Ephesians 5:21–33

What does God want us to see in the marriage of a husband and wife? God created marriage to be a picture of Christ and the church. As a wife respects and submits to her husband, and as a husband lovingly leads and makes sacrifices for his wife, a human marriage can be a living parable of Christ and the church. Christ loved us and gave Himself to be sacrificed on the cross for us. And we respond to Christ's sacrificial love with respect and submission.

TALK ABOUT IT

Who created marriage?

What is marriage a picture of? And how?

What do we learn in this passage about Christ's love for the church?

Read Ephesians 6:1–4

What does it mean that children are to obey their parents "in the Lord" (v. 1)? It means children are obeying Jesus when they obey their parents. God loves children so much He gave them parents who would teach them to obey. When children learn to obey their parents, they learn to obey God. There are three reasons children are to obey their parents. The first is that it is "right." If your mother says to clean your room, then you clean your room. If your father says to walk the dog, then you walk the dog. It is wrong to disobey your parents. The second reason is that obedience "honors" parents. You honor your parents when you obey with your heart as well as by what you do. You honor your mother when you cheerfully set the table and don't complain when she asks. The third reason comes from the promise "that it may go well with you" (v. 3). Like an umbrella protects us from the rain, parents protect us from harm. An obedient child knows the joy of God's blessing (Prov. 3:1–4).

TALK ABOUT IT

What does it mean to obey your parents in the Lord?

What are some blessings that will come as you obey your parents?

How do you plan to honor, as well as obey, your parents?

Read Ephesians 6:10–20

Why are we told to be "strong in the Lord" (v. 10)? We are told this because we have a powerful enemy. While God's children live in this world, they will have an enemy called Satan. God created Satan as an angel of light. But Satan chose to be evil, and God threw him out of heaven. Now Satan tries to get people to doubt, lie, steal, cheat, and everything else God hates. The only way for us to fight Satan is to be "strong in the Lord and in the strength of his might" (v. 1). Just like a soldier trains his body to be strong for battle, we are to train our minds and hearts, so we are strong to fight the spiritual battle. Our minds and hearts become strong as we read God's Word and follow His will. God gives His children special armor.

TALK ABOUT IT

How do we become strong in the Lord?

What are the pieces of armor we need to put on?

Why do we need this armor?

Prayer

Father God, thank You for the amazing free gift of salvation in Christ. We praise You for Your abundant grace and mercy that saves us not because of what we've done, but because of who You are. Thank You for redeeming us from the penalty of sin. Help us to live by the power of the Holy Spirit, bringing glory and honor to You.

PHILIPPIANS

Introduction

Paul wrote this letter to the Christians in the city of Philippi. Paul was in jail in Rome when he wrote this letter. But even though Paul was imprisoned at this time, Christian *joy* is one of the main themes of the letter. Acts 16 tells us how the church in Philippi began, with the amazing stories of Lydia and the Philippian jailer.

ICEBREAKER: Can you think of someone in your life who is an amazing volunteer or servant? Tell us about them.

Read Philippians 1:1–14

Why was Paul joyful? Paul was in prison when he wrote this letter. How could he have joy while in jail? Paul's joy came from the Lord, not from having a comfortable life. Even though Paul's life was very difficult, he rejoiced that God is always good. And God is working in the world to spread the gospel far and wide. God was even using Paul's imprisonment as a way for people to hear about Jesus (see vv. 12–14). It is obvious from these verses that Paul cared very much for the believers in Philippi. He loved them and wanted them to continue growing in their relationship with the Lord. Paul was confident that God, who started a good work in them, would keep them all the way until Jesus comes back. And Paul prayed that their love would grow, with knowledge and discernment, all to the glory and praise of God.

TALK ABOUT IT

How could Paul feel joy even while he was in prison?

In what ways does Paul express his affection for the believers in Philippi?

How can you turn Paul's prayer into a prayer for your own spiritual growth?

Read Philippians 2:1–11

What does it mean to be humble? God wants us to think of others more than we think of ourselves. If we're selfish and prideful, we will think that our wants and our accomplishments are most important. But if we're humble and others-centered, we will focus on the needs and interests of others. Jesus is the ultimate example of humility. He left His home in heaven to come and be a servant in our fallen world. He even humbled Himself to a shameful and agonizing death on a Roman cross. Jesus is our Savior and Lord. We can pray for the Spirit to help us become more humble, willing to make sacrifices in order to serve others. After Jesus humbled Himself to the point of crucifixion, God then raised Jesus up to a place of glory and honor. Eventually everyone will acknowledge that Jesus Christ is Lord, to the glory of God the Father. This is our great Savior. He is the perfect example of humility, and He will be our eternal King. He went down, down, down to serve us. Then God the Father raised Jesus up, up, up, for everyone to see how great He is.

TALK ABOUT IT

How do these verses describe Jesus going down, down, down, and then up, up, up?

What did it mean for Jesus to be humble?

What will it look like for you to be humble?

Prayer

Jesus, we praise You that You are the ultimate example of humility. Thank You for Your obedience to the Father, to the point of death on a cross. You set an example for us in sacrificing Yourself for the good of others. Help us to put others' needs above our own. Help us to have humble hearts that honor You.

COLOSSIANS

Introduction

Colossians is another one of Paul's "prison letters." Paul (with the help of Timothy) wrote this letter to the church in Colossae, while Paul was in jail in Rome (around the same time Paul wrote Ephesians, Philippians, and Philemon, which are the other "prison letters"). There were some bad teachers in Colossae who were teaching wrong things about how to follow Jesus. Paul wrote this letter to guard the believers from the dangers of these false teachings.

ICEBREAKER: If you could get first place in anything, what would it be?

Read Colossians 1:11–23

Jesus is first place! What is it like to win first place in a competition? It means you're the best, or the smartest, or the fastest, or the strongest. The Bible tells us that Jesus is first place in the universe. Jesus is the beloved Son of God the Father. And the Father made Jesus to be preeminent (first place!) over all creation. Jesus is also the image of the invisible God. God the Father is invisible. Jesus, who is fully God as the second person of the Trinity, became visible when He came to earth as a human being. Jesus is the One who can save us from our sins.

TALK ABOUT IT

In what ways is Jesus first place?

How is Jesus the image of the invisible God?

What can you do to honor Jesus for being first place?

Prayer

Jesus, we praise You that You are first place! You are over all creation, the image of the invisible God, and the Creator and Sustainer of all things. Help us to continue in the faith, stable and steadfast.

1 & 2 THESSALONIANS

Introduction

These are letters Paul wrote to the church in the city of Thessalonica. Paul wrote these letters with the help of Silvanus and Timothy. The believers in Thessalonica had not been Christians for very long, and there were others in their city who were mean to them because of their faith (Acts 17:1–9; 1 Thess. 1:6; 2:14; 2 Thess. 1:4). Paul wrote these letters to encourage them and to instruct them on various things, especially about the second coming of Christ.

1 Thessalonians

ICEBREAKER: What is something that you're looking forward to in the future?

Read 1 Thessalonians 4:13–18

What will happen when Jesus comes back? Paul wanted the believers in Thessalonica to know what to expect in the future. When Paul talks about those who have fallen asleep, he means Christians who have died. When Jesus returns, the dead in Christ will rise first. Then the believers who have not died will be gathered together with them to meet Jesus in the sky. It will be an amazing day! And from that day forward, those who have trusted in Jesus will be with Him always. Knowing what will happen when Jesus comes back gives us hope. When a beloved Christian dies, we can grieve with hope. We're sad that they're no longer with us. But we can be encouraged, knowing they are with the Lord. And we don't need to be afraid to die, if we are trusting in the Lord. Because all Christians can look forward to being with Jesus forever and ever in heaven.

TALK ABOUT IT

What are some things we will hear when Jesus comes back (see verse 16)?

What did Paul want the Thessalonian church to understand?

How will this information help them, and us?

Prayer

Lord, we praise You that You're coming back! Death does not have the final say. We thank You for the promise that those who know You will be with You in heaven. Help us not to fear death but to know we have hope for eternity because of Jesus.

2 Thessalonians

ICEBREAKER: What makes you feel ready or prepared for a big change?

Read 2 Thessalonians 1:5–12

What will happen when Jesus comes back? The believers in Thessalonica were being persecuted because of their faith in Jesus. Paul wanted them to know that Jesus will bring justice. It's not fair when people do bad things to Christians. If those people never ask Jesus to forgive them, they will be punished by Jesus when He returns. And their punishment will be eternal. When Jesus comes a second time, it will be a day of rejoicing for everyone who is a follower of Jesus. At the same time, it will be a day of shock and sadness for everyone who refused to follow Jesus. It's important that we live in a way that we're ready for Jesus' return. And we should do what we can to help others be ready too.

TALK ABOUT IT

What does it mean to be fair, or just?

How will the Lord's judgment bring justice in the end?

What can you do to be ready for Jesus to come back?

Prayer

Father God, we praise You that You are a God of justice. You are our avenger and will make all things right. Help us to be ready for Your return, to boldly share our faith with those who don't know You. Help us to live in a way that is worthy of Your calling.

1 & 2 TIMOTHY

Introduction

Paul wrote these letters to Timothy, who was like a son to Paul, a son in the faith. Timothy was a leader in the church in Ephesus, and Timothy needed some guidance from Paul about how to lead the church. The second letter Paul wrote to Timothy (2 Tim.) was written by Paul shortly before Paul was executed.

1 Timothy

ICEBREAKER: Do you have a favorite toy or game? What is it?

Read 1 Timothy 3:1–13

Who are the leaders in the local church? In this passage, Paul instructs Timothy about two important roles. Pastors (also referred to as elders or overseers) and deacons are part of God's design for His church. Pastors and elders teach and lead the church. Deacons serve in a variety of ways (see Acts 6, for an example). A person needs to meet these qualifications before they can be appointed to one of these positions. A pastor must be able to teach God's Word. And just as important, a pastor needs to live in humility and holiness according to God's Word. The requirements for deacons are very similar. Really the only difference is that deacons don't need to be able to teach. But pastors and deacons, alike, must be mature and godly believers who are examples to the rest of the believers in the church.

TALK ABOUT IT

What are the qualifications for pastors/elders/overseers?

What are the qualifications for deacons?

Who are the pastors and deacons in your congregation? How can you pray for them?

Read 1 Timothy 6:6–19

What does it mean to be content? Are you happy with what you have? Or do you find yourself thinking a lot about the things you don't have? Are there toys, games, privileges, or abilities that your friends have that you wish you had? God wants us to enjoy the good things He has given us. He doesn't want us to always be gloomy because of the things we don't have. Think about it. When you were born, you didn't bring anything into the world with you. And when you die, you won't take anything out of the world. If you have food to eat, clothes to wear, and a roof over your head, you can thank God for these blessings. You can focus on growing in your relationship with Jesus instead of focusing on trying to get more and more stuff. We should want to be rich in the truest sense. We should want to be rich in good works, storing up treasure in heaven.

TALK ABOUT IT

What is contentment? What is discontentment?

What is dangerous about the love of money?

In what ways are you tempted to be discontented?

Prayer

God, we praise You that You are the giver of all good gifts. Thank You for blessing us with all that we need and more. Forgive us when we envy what others have. Help us to be content with the good gifts You've given us. Give us a grateful heart that counts the blessings in our lives.

2 Timothy

ICEBREAKER: Who is your favorite teacher? Why?

Read 2 Timothy 1:1–5; 3:14–17

Who wrote the Bible? In this letter Paul is writing to Timothy, who was like a son to him. Timothy learned about God from his grandmother Lois and his mother Eunice. Paul encourages Timothy to continue in what they taught him. Then Paul teaches us something very important about the Scriptures. All Scripture is breathed out (inspired) by God. This means that God breathed out all the words of Scripture through human authors, like Moses, David, Luke, and Paul. Everything we read in the Bible is ultimately from God. We can believe that what the Bible teaches is true. We can trust that what the Bible says about Jesus will lead us to eternal life. And we must obey the words of Scripture as God's commands for how we ought to live.

TALK ABOUT IT

Who wrote the Bible?

How is the Bible different from any other book?

Name some things in the Bible we need to trust and obey.

Prayer

Father God, we praise You for breathing out all the words of the Bible. Your words are true and can be trusted. We thank You for giving us faithful teachers who instruct us in Your Word, like Timothy's grandma, Lois, and mom, Eunice, did for him. Help us to diligently study Your Word and live out its message.

TITUS

Introduction

Paul wrote this letter to a man named Titus, who was a leader in the church, similar to Timothy.

ICEBREAKER: Have you ever needed to be in charge of something? What was it like?

Read Titus 1:1–9

Here is another letter Paul wrote to a younger man whom he considered to be a son in the faith. Titus was a leader in the early church, and he needed Paul's encouragement. Paul needed Titus to defend the truth and protect churches from false teachers. Paul was a church planter. After he planted some churches in Crete, Paul left Titus there to help lead those churches to maturity. In this short letter, Paul instructs Titus about who should lead the church and about wrong teachings that threaten to harm the church.

TALK ABOUT IT

How does Paul describe himself in the greeting/opening of the letter? How does Paul describe Titus?

How do these elder qualifications compare to the ones in 1 Timothy 3?

What were the people like who were threatening to harm the church? What are some wrong teachings that harm the church today?

Prayer

Lord, thank You for faithful servants, like Paul and Titus, who have gone before us. Thank You for our church leaders. Please guard our churches from false teachers and help bring order, peace, and a zeal for the gospel to our body of believers.

PHILEMON

Introduction

Paul wrote this letter to his Philemon. It's a letter with a wonderful theme of forgiveness.

ICEBREAKER: Name something that is easy to forgive. Name something that is hard to forgive.

Read Philemon 1:1–25

What did Paul want Philemon to do? Paul and Philemon were friends. More than that, they were brothers in Christ. At this time, Paul was in prison because of his faith in Christ. While in prison, Paul met Onesimus. Onesimus was a slave in the home of Philemon. But Onesimus ran away. Paul sends Onesimus back to Philemon with this letter. Paul wants Philemon and Onesimus to be friends. More than that, he wants them to act like brothers in Christ. No longer master and slave. Jesus paid the debt we owe for our sins against God. We can forgive others for the ways they've sinned against us.

TALK ABOUT IT

What is slavery? Why is it wrong?

Who was Philemon? Who was Onesimus?

How does Jesus' forgiveness of us help us to forgive others?

Prayer

Our Father in heaven, we pray for all those who are in bondage. Please set them free. And forgive us our debts and help us to forgive those who are in debt to us.

HEBREWS

Introduction

We're not sure who wrote this letter, but we know the author was a friend of Timothy (see Heb. 13:23). The author of this amazing letter was someone who knew the Old Testament very well and was writing to a group of Christians with a Jewish background. This letter shows us how Jesus is the fulfillment of the Old Testament.

> ICEBREAKER: **Name an athlete who is really good at their sport. Then name another athlete who is even better.**

Read Hebrews 3:1–19

Who is greater than Moses? Jesus is greater than Moses! That's not a put-down to Moses. It just shows that Jesus is the main hero of the Bible. Moses was one of the main heroes of the Old Testament. God used Moses in powerful ways to lead the Israelites out of slavery. Jesus is God's own Son, so He gets way more glory than Moses. The writer of Hebrews teaches us a lot about the Old Testament and how the things in the Old Testament point us to Jesus. The book of Hebrews also has important warnings for us to hear. Like in Hebrews 3:12–13: Sin is deceitful. Temptations lie to us, telling us that life will be fun and exciting if we disobey God. This is why we need one another. We need other followers of Jesus to remind us, and even correct us, if we're letting sin lead us astray.

TALK ABOUT IT

Jesus is greater than _______ [fill in the blank with several Old Testament "heroes"].

Read Hebrews 3:3 again. What does the illustration about the house and builder teach you?

Think of some ways you can remind one another about the deceitfulness of sin.

Prayer

Lord Jesus, we praise You as the One who is greater than angels and greater than Moses. Thank You for being our Great High Priest. Please help us to be on guard against the lies of sin.

JAMES

Introduction

This letter was written by James, who was a brother of Jesus. James became a follower of Jesus, and a leader in the early church. James wrote this letter to teach Christians how to put their faith into action. In some ways, this New Testament letter is similar to the Old Testament book of Proverbs.

ICEBREAKER: When you look in a mirror, what do you see? What do you notice about yourself?

Read James 1:19–27

Have you ever looked in a mirror and realized there is food stuck between your teeth? What do you do? Fix it, right? The gospel is similar. Reading God's Word shows us what's true about ourselves and helps us to know what needs to change in our lives. James was Jesus' half-brother and a leader in the church at Jerusalem. He wanted the Jewish Christians to know that hearing God's Word is not enough. We also need to be "doers of the word" (v. 22). What is hearing God's Word but not putting it into practice like? That is like a person who looks in a mirror and walks away, forgetting what they look like! True faith in Jesus comes by grace and always leads to action—like caring for widows or orphans, people who have no one to care for them. James 2 tells us that faith without works is dead, or useless. That means that our faith is proven true by our words *and* our actions. If a person is cold or hungry, don't just wish them well. Give them a blanket and food! God loves us and accepts us not because of our good deeds but because of our faith in him. But our good deeds show that our faith is real.

TALK ABOUT IT

What does it mean to be not just a hearer of the word but a doer of the word?

What example does James give us of a pure and undefiled religion?

What is one practical way you can show your faith by what you do?

Prayer

Lord, thank You that You love me not because of what I do, but because of Your amazing grace. Help me show my faith to others by my actions and words. Help me to be not just a hearer of the word but a doer of the word.

1 & 2 PETER

Introduction

These letters were written by Peter, one of the twelve disciples and a close friend and follower of Jesus. Peter wrote these letters to be sent to churches throughout a number of provinces of the Roman Empire. A major theme in these letters is the suffering that Christians will face in this life.

1 Peter

ICEBREAKER: Talk about a time when you had to persevere through something difficult. What motivated you to keep going?

Read 1 Peter 4:12–16

Peter was one of Jesus' twelve disciples. He was a fisherman. He and his brother Andrew left their nets to follow Jesus. Peter wrote his letter to followers of Jesus who were experiencing persecution and suffering. They were being mistreated because of their faith. Some even had to leave their homes and move to different cities. Peter wanted to remind them that as Christians, we are to have an upside-down view of suffering. For example, we can rejoice when we suffer because we're sharing in Christ's sufferings. We are experiencing a tiny bit of what He experienced. We are blessed when we are made fun of or persecuted for Christ's name because his Spirit rests on us. We don't need to be ashamed as God is proud of us for being true to Him in hard times. Our hope is in heaven.

TALK ABOUT IT

Why were Jesus' followers being mistreated?

How should our view of suffering be different as Christians?

How can you persevere through something hard you're experiencing?

Prayer

Father God, You give us everything we need to endure hard things. Help us not to give up but to put our hope in You. Help us to persevere and stay true to Your word even during hard times. We love you.

2 Peter

ICEBREAKER: What's a job that requires hard work and perseverance?

Read 2 Peter 1:3–8

Peter was a leader in the early church. He wanted to encourage other believers that God equips us for the hard things we go through. We become "partakers of the divine nature" (v. 4) by the Holy Spirit living in us. The Holy Spirit reveals to us when we sin, comforts us, and helps us remember God's truth. When you memorize a Bible verse, it's the Holy Spirit who will help you recall it at just the right time. He will help you grow in godliness, knowledge of the Lord, and love for others. The Holy Spirit used Peter to comfort and encourage the church during hard times. He wanted them to know that God would help them become more like Jesus as they endured suffering.

TALK ABOUT IT

What does God promise to give us? How will that help us live a life that's pleasing to Him?

Even though we depend on the Holy Spirit to equip us, we also play a part in growing more like Jesus. How can we grow even through difficult times?

Do you know someone walking through persecution or difficulty? How can you pray for them?

Prayer

Lord Jesus, we praise You that You give us everything we need to live a life that's pleasing to You. Help us not to waver in our faith or give up when we're feeling discouraged. Help us to depend on Your Holy Spirit to comfort us and remind us of truth. Let us be a light of hope and grace to others, pointing them to You.

1, 2, 3 JOHN

Introduction

These letters were written by the same John who wrote the gospel of John and the book of Revelation. John has a different writing style than Paul. It's helpful to learn from different teachers who are all explaining the same good news about Jesus. God inspired a variety of writers to record the truths we need to know about God, sin, and salvation.

1 John

ICEBREAKER: What is something that you know for sure? What is something that you doubt?

Read 1 John 1:1–10

How do you know that something is real and true? The book of 1 John is all about knowing with full assurance that we are Christians. John reminds us at the start of his letter that he has seen Jesus! He not only has seen Him with his eyes—he's touched Him, heard Him, and been with Him. Jesus is eternal life in bodily form. Isn't it cool that God wanted us to have a visible representation of eternal life? John wants us to know Jesus too. One way of knowing that we are true Christians is by walking with Jesus in obedience to His Word. He is light and there is no darkness, or sin, in Him. We are promised that if we confess our sins, He is faithful to forgive us! Isn't that an amazing promise? But if we claim to be without sin, we make Him a liar and prove not to be real Christians. What would you say? How do you know that you really know Jesus?

TALK ABOUT IT

What evidence does John give that he truly knows Jesus?

What is John's purpose in writing the letter?

How do we know that we are truly Christians? What promise does God give us?

Read 1 John 3:16–24

How do we know what love really is? John answers that question in our reading today. Jesus is the ultimate example of love as He laid down His life for us, dying on the cross for our sins. He sets an example for us in loving others. Jesus didn't show love only in His words to us, but in His actions. In the same way, we need to show our love for others by serving them, meeting their needs, and being willing to make a sacrifice for them (like handing over the biggest slice of cake to your sibling!). When we love like Jesus does, He gives us confidence that we really know Him. We can be sure that He hears our prayers and answers them according to His will. What an amazing promise! When we believe in Jesus and love those around us, we are obeying God's commands. He gives us His Holy Spirit to live inside us and help us abide, or trust, in Him.

TALK ABOUT IT

How do we know what love is according to this passage?

What will give us confidence before God as we pray?

How can you show love to someone today?

Prayer

Heavenly Father, we're so thankful that You sent Your son to live a perfect life on earth. We're grateful for Your Word that reminds us that Jesus is real and true. Help us to walk in the light and be quick to confess our sins. Let us rejoice in the eternal life You give us in Jesus!

2 John

ICEBREAKER: Have you ever been tricked or deceived by someone? What happened?

Read 2 John 1:4–11

John finds great joy in that some of his children are walking in God's ways. He reminds us that we love one another by obeying God's commands and living out the truth of His Word. Maybe this looks like sitting by the new kid at lunchtime who doesn't have many friends, or offering to help set the table at dinner. But he also gives us a warning: There are deceivers in the world who don't know Jesus and don't obey His teaching. We need to be careful not to fall into their traps, becoming blind to our sin. Can you think of some ways the world might try to deceive us? John promises us that when we abide in the teaching of Christ, we have both the Son and the Father. We are known and loved by God.

TALK ABOUT IT

How does John describe love?

What does John warn us about? Why?

How will you be watchful over your own heart and life?

Prayer

Lord, thank You that Your Word is truth. Thank You for affirming that we know You when we walk in Your truth. Help us to beware of the deceivers in the world. Give us discernment to judge truth from error, evil from good. Protect our hearts and minds as we seek to honor You.

3 John

ICEBREAKER: What is something that gives you great joy?

Read 3 John 1:1–15

John tells us that he has no greater joy than to hear that his children are walking in the truth. He desires for the church to send these brothers on their missionary journey, in a manner worthy of God. He desires for the church to be generous in meeting their needs, so they can be fellow workers alongside them. Yet there is danger in the camp! A man named Diotrephes, who likes to put himself first, does not acknowledge the apostles' authority. He is saying bad, untrue things about them to others. He is not welcoming anyone who follows Jesus. John gives them a loving warning not to imitate evil but good. At the end of the letter, John mentions hoping to talk to them face-to-face. Why do you think seeing each other face-to-face is important?

TALK ABOUT IT

What is John's greatest joy?

What would it mean to send the brothers out in a manner worthy of God?

What would it look like to put yourself first? What is one way you can avoid selfishness and put others first?

Prayer

God, help us to walk in the truth. Convict our hearts when we act in pride or selfishness. Protect us from evil and cause us to imitate what is good.

JUDE

Introduction

This letter was written by Jude, who was a brother of Jesus (and a brother of James). Like James, Jude became a follower of Jesus. Jude wrote this letter to encourage Christians and warn them not to be deceived by false teachers.

ICEBREAKER: Have you ever had to stand up for what is right and true? Tell us about it.

Read Jude 1:17–23

Jude, one of Jesus' younger half-brothers, wanted other Christians to stand up for what God says is right and true. He warned the church that some false teachers would cause division in the church and try to dissuade Christians from following the truth. They made ungodly choices and lived however they wanted, sinning against God. These people did not have the Holy Spirit living in them. Yet believers need to remember the predictions of the apostles of Christ. They need to encourage one another in the faith and let the Holy Spirit guide them in their prayers. Jude wants them to be merciful toward those who doubt their faith and rescue unbelievers from their sinful choices, pointing them to Jesus. Jesus is able to keep us from sin. Rely on Him.

TALK ABOUT IT

Why was Jude concerned for the church?

What characterizes false teachers?

How can we keep drawing closer to Jesus?

Prayer

Thank You, Lord, for the warnings You give us in Scripture. Help my eyes to discern good from evil, truth from error. Please protect our church from false teachers and keep me growing in godliness, unafraid to stand for truth.

REVELATION

Introduction

This last book of the New Testament was written by the same John who wrote the gospel of John, and the letters of 1, 2, 3 John. This is a very unique book. Some would call it strange! John received visions from Jesus about heavenly happenings, including things that will take place in the future. Even though there may be many parts of this book that are difficult to understand, we should understand this: Jesus wins! And those who trust Him will be with Him in heaven forever!

ICEBREAKER: What do you think heaven will be like?

Read Revelation 1:1–11

Who is John? God is the author, and John is the person God used to write the book of Revelation. John, one of Jesus' closest friends, lived at a time when people who worshiped Jesus were hated. John himself was on the island of Patmos as punishment for telling people about Jesus. Through John, God gave this message to encourage His servants. They needed to know Jesus' love for us is so great that He died to free us from sin. And Jesus loves you! As you believe in Jesus, you are forgiven of sin so you can live for God.

TALK ABOUT IT

Why did God give the message of Revelation to the people?

What did Jesus do to show His great love for us?

How has Jesus' love for you made a difference in your life?

Read Revelation 1:12–20

What did John see? God gave John a special vision of Jesus dressed like a royal King. His hair was very white, and His eyes seemed like fire. His feet glowed like hot metal, and when He spoke it was like the powerful sound of a huge waterfall. Out of Jesus' mouth came a sword, sharpened on both sides. And His face was like looking at the sun. Jesus showed John His majesty and power in a different way from when Jesus was on earth. John worshiped Jesus as the majestic King of the universe. Jesus brings life to those who believe.

TALK ABOUT IT

What did God show John about Jesus?

What did John do when he saw Jesus as the majestic King?

How is this description of Jesus different than what we read in the Gospels?

Read Revelation 4:1–11

What did John see next? God let John see into heaven to know what He will do in the future. John saw God on His throne. God is strong and rules over the entire universe. He is greater than any king, president, or prime minister on earth. God's throne is surrounded by the thrones of twenty-four wise rulers who honor God. When John heard thunder and saw the seven blazing torches, he knew God is the One who has complete power over the world. If we want to understand what will happen in the future, we must think most of all of God's complete power. God is in control, and He is working all things toward good.

TALK ABOUT IT

What did God let John see and know?

What do we learn about worship in this passage?

How can you worship God?

Read Revelation 5:1–10

What did John learn about the scroll? John learned that the only person able to open the scroll to find out God's plan for the future is Jesus. Jesus is the King God promised to send, to save the people from their sins. John looked for this King, but instead he saw a Lamb. Jesus is called the Lamb of God. Before Jesus, lambs were offered as sacrifices when people confessed their sins to God and asked for forgiveness. The lambs took the punishment for sin and the sinner was forgiven. Jesus is the perfect Lamb, who died to take the punishment for our sins.

TALK ABOUT IT

Who was the only person able to open the scroll?

Why is Jesus called the Lamb of God?

What makes Jesus "worthy"? What does that mean?

Read Revelation 5:11–14

What did John see in the throne room of God? He saw the room fill up with thousands and thousands of angels. They were singing that Jesus is worthy of all honor and praise. People who give their life for the freedom of their country deserve to be honored. But how much more, Jesus, who died so you can be saved and live as God's child forever! Then John saw all of creation—mountains, trees, lions, tigers, stars, men, women, and children—join the angels in worship of Jesus. Jesus alone is worthy of the worship of all creation.

TALK ABOUT IT

Why is Jesus worthy of the worship of all creation?

What are some things you love?

How can you show Jesus that you love Him? What words can you say to honor Him?

Read Revelation 19:1–10

What did John hear in heaven? John heard the roar of a huge crowd praising God. They praised God for His power to save His people from evil. Babylon was destroyed! Then the great crowd praised God because of the wedding of the Lamb. The Lamb is the Lord Jesus Christ. He is called the Lamb because He died as a sacrifice to take the punishment for our sins. In this picture of a wedding, Jesus the Lamb is the "groom," or husband, and His people are together called His "bride." The wedding pictures the wonderful celebration. Jesus will return and be joined with His people forever.

TALK ABOUT IT

Why did the huge crowd praise God?

Think of wedding celebrations you've attended and compare it to what will happen when Jesus returns.

How much do you look forward to Jesus' return?

Read Revelation 19:11–21

What did John see before him on a white horse? John called the rider Faithful and True. He is Jesus. Jesus always keeps His promises. And

He will return, just as He said. John said He had a name no one knew – because Jesus as God's Son is greater than we can understand. He was wearing a robe like a king. The edge of the robe was dipped in blood. We remember Jesus died on the cross for us. Another name for Him is the Word of God. With the power of a sharp sword, Jesus speaks God's Word and is God's Word. He is King of kings and Lord of lords. King Jesus will return and rule the world.

TALK ABOUT IT

Why is Jesus called Faithful and True? Why is He called King of kings and Lord of lords?

What does it mean that Jesus is the Word of God?

Who will need to be afraid of Jesus when He comes in the way this passage describes?

Read Revelation 20:1–6

What did John see an angel holding? The angel held a key and a chain. The key opened a bottomless hole called the pit. Satan (that ancient serpent) was chained and put in the pit for a thousand years. Satan will not be able to tell lies and lead people to believe what is not true. Next, John saw the resurrection of God's people. God's people are given new bodies, like Jesus' new body after He died on the cross. God's people will be given a new body to reign with King Jesus.

TALK ABOUT IT

Why is Satan described as a serpent?

What will happen to Satan? What will happen to God's people?

How can we avoid being deceived by Satan?

Prayer

God, I praise You for being in control of the universe. You will destroy Satan, so he cannot tell lies any more. Thank You for the promise, as a believer in Jesus Christ, that my body will rise and I will reign with Jesus when He returns. Please help me live for Jesus today.

Read Revelation 21:9–14

What did John see coming from heaven? God let John see the Holy City. This is what we call heaven, where God's children will live forever. God's children are called "the bride" of the Lamb—Jesus Christ. Only Jesus can wash away our sin and free us to live with God forever. The Holy City shines brightly, not with lights, but with God. God is a million times brighter than the sun. A great, high wall surrounds the Holy City. All God's children are secure in His love and protection forever. God will live with His children forever.

TALK ABOUT IT

What is the place God has made for His children to live with Him?

Why is the Holy City so bright?

What will heaven be like based on John's vision? What about it is wonderful and exciting to you?

Read Revelation 22:1–5

What did the angel show John? The angel showed John "the river of the water of life" (v. 1). Along the side of the river, John saw the tree of life. The tree of life is so full of life that it produces fruit every month. God gives His children this fruit to show that they have new life with Him forever. This is like in the garden of Eden, before sin came into the world. But this is even better! God will have many good gifts to give us, and He will abundantly provide for us throughout eternity. In the Holy City, God's children will enjoy being with God. They will be so happy to love God and serve Him. God's children will love being with Him.

TALK ABOUT IT

What grows alongside the river?

How long will God's children live with Him?

Why do you think God's children love being with Him?

Read Revelation 22:10–21

What did the angel tell John? The angel told John that Jesus will come back soon. To think we can be ready for Jesus sometime later, is not right. To be ready for Jesus is to turn from sin and trust Him, now! Jesus changes our heart. Jesus rewards us by giving us Himself. He gives us the gift of living with God forever. Those who refuse to turn from sin and trust in Jesus will not enter the Holy City of God. Jesus is the only one who can give us the gift of living with God forever.

TALK ABOUT IT

Who is coming back soon?

What does it mean to be ready for Jesus?

How ready are you for Jesus' return?

Prayer

Heavenly Father, You are almighty and sovereign over life and death. Thank You for sending Jesus to die on a cross so that I might be forgiven of my sin. Please give me faith to turn away from my sin and trust in You. I want to be with You forever. Help me to be ready for Your return.

IN CLOSING

We hope these Bible readings and discussion questions have been a blessing to you and your family. God's Word is powerful!

Our prayer is that God will use parents to instill in their children a deep respect and love for biblical truth. As kids experience the habit of regular interaction with Scripture, we pray for the Holy Spirit to awaken in them spiritual curiosity leading to salvation and a lifelong devotion to the Lord Jesus.

To God be the glory!

APPENDIX: SUGGESTED READINGS

Here we've included some suggested readings on various topics, on several attributes of God, and for certain seasons of the year. The topical section could be used when teachable moments come up in the life of your family. The adventure stories could pair well with family vacation. In the weeks leading up to Christmas and Easter, your family could focus on the readings related to those key biblical events.

Readings on Special Topics

Anxiety / Worry: Luke 12:22–29

Complaining / Contentment: Exodus 16:1–18; Numbers 21:4–9; Psalm 95; 1 Timothy 6:6–19

Conviction of Sin / Repentance: Genesis 42:6–17; Matthew 3:7–12; Luke 18:9–14; Acts 2:36–40

Courage: Deuteronomy 31:1–8; Joshua 1:3–9; Judges 4:1–23; Daniel 3:8–30; Daniel 6:10–28

Discipleship / Following Jesus: Mark 1:16–20; John 3:1–8; Mark 6:7–13, Mark 8:34–38; Luke 10:25–37; Luke 14:25–33, Matthew 28:16–20

Forgiveness: 2 Samuel 12:1–10, 13–14; Matthew 18:21–27; Matthew 18:28–35; Philemon 1:1–25

Friendship: 1 Samuel 20:12–17; John 13:1–17

Generosity / Money: Luke 12:13–21; Luke 18:18–30; 2 Corinthians 8:1–9; 2 Corinthians 9:6–15

Humility: Mark 10:35–45; John 13:1–17; Philippians 2:1–11

Jealousy: Genesis 37:1–11; Genesis 37:18–36; 1 Samuel 18:6–9, 12–16; Matthew 20:1–16

Obedience: Joshua 1:10–18; Jonah 1–2; Ephesians 6:1–4; James 1:19–27

Prayer: Joshua 10:7–15; 1 Samuel 1:9–11, 20, 24–28; 2 Samuel 7:18–29; Luke 2:36–40; Ephesians 1:15–23; Ephesians 3

Salvation: Acts 2:36–40; Romans 4:1–12; Galatians 2:11–21; Ephesians 2:1–10

Suffering: Genesis 50:18–21; Job 1:1–22; Job 2:1–10; Job 38:1–4; Job 40:1–8; Job 42:1–17; Psalm 69:1–18; Acts 5:17–20, 27–33, 40–42; Romans 5:1–11

Temptation: Genesis 3:4–6; 2 Samuel 11:1–5; Matthew 4:1–4; Matthew 4:5–11; Acts 5:1–11

Worship: Judges 5:1–3; 2 Samuel 22:1–7; Nehemiah 8:1–8; Isaiah 6; Revelation 4:1–11; Revelation 5:1–10; Revelation 5:11–14

Readings on the Attributes of God

God as Creator: Genesis 1:1–2; Genesis 1:3–5; Genesis 1:6–13; Genesis 1:20–25; Genesis 1:26–28; John 1:1–18; Romans 1:18–21

God's Faithfulness: Genesis 12:2–3; Genesis 50:18–21; Revelation 19:11–21

God's Grace: Hosea 1:2–11; 3:1–5; Luke 18:9–14; Romans 5:12–19; Ephesians 2:1–10

God's Holiness: Leviticus 1:1–9; 2:1–3; 3:1–2; 5:14–16; Leviticus 16:1–22; 2 Samuel 6:1–15; Isaiah 6

God's Justice / Judgment: Jeremiah 12:1–17; Amos 5:6–24; Romans 1:22–32; Romans 2:5–16; 2 Thessalonians 1:5–12

God's Love: Hosea 1:2–11; 3:1–5; Romans 8:31–39; Ephesians 2:1–10

God's Omnipotence / Power: Genesis 1:1–2; Joshua 10:7–15; Jonah 1–2; Matthew 1:18–20; Ephesians 1:1–14; Ephesians 3

God's Sovereignty: Genesis 41:25–32; Genesis 50:18–21; Romans 8:28–30; Romans 8:31–39; Romans 9:1–18

Adventure Stories

Numbers 13:1–3, 25–33; Numbers 14:26–31; Joshua 2:1–7; Joshua 2:8–16; Joshua 2:17–24; Judges 4:1–23; Judges 7:1–22; 1 Samuel 24:1–20; Daniel 3:8–30; Daniel 6:10–28; Jonah 1–2; Jonah 3–4

Readings for Christmas

Micah 5:1–6; Luke 1:5–7, 11–17; Luke 1:26–38; Matthew 1:18–20; Matthew 1:21–25; Luke 1:39–45; Luke 1:46–56; Luke 1:57–66; Luke 2:1–7; Luke 2:8–14; Luke 2:15–20; John 1:1–18; Matthew 2:1–12; Luke 2:21–35; Luke 2:36–40; Luke 2:41–52; Philippians 2:1–11

Readings for Easter

Genesis 22:1–14; Exodus 12:1–14, 24–27; Exodus 13:8–9; Isaiah 52:13–53:12; Zechariah 9:9–17; John 11:1–44; Mark 10:32–24; John 13:1–17; Mark 14:10–21; Mark 14:27–31; Luke 22:7–16; Luke 22:17–23; Mark 14:43–52; Mark 14:55–65; Mark 15:1–15; Luke 23:33–38; Luke 23:39–43; Luke 23:44–49; Matthew 28:1–6; Matthew 28:7–10; Luke 24:1–8; Luke 24:9–11; Luke 24:13–24; Luke 24:25–27; Luke 24:30–32; Matthew 28:16–20; Acts 1:3–5; Acts 1:8–11

ACKNOWLEDGMENTS

This book would not be possible without the vision and heart of Barbara Reaoch. Barb's love for God's word spilled over into everything she did. She discipled her own children—teaching my husband inductive Bible study methods while he was in high school—and taught thousands of women through Bible Study Fellowship. She also wrote BSF children's curriculum and family devotionals for Christmas and Easter that are now used around the world. Her passion to pass on her faith to the next generation was evident through all of it. *The Word in Our Home* was her final writing dream—a family devotional through every book of the Bible. Even in the midst of fighting ovarian cancer, she was planning how to make her dream a reality. In her final weeks of life on this earth, Barb shared with Ben the files and drafts of many of the devotions you read. With the help of Moody Publishers, Ben and I were able to pick up the baton to complete the work that Barb had begun.

We're incredibly thankful for our acquisitions editor, Catherine Parks, who helped make this dream a reality, as well as Amanda Cleary Eastep's excellent editing skills. We're grateful for the marketing team at Moody, including Erica Dvorak and Janis Backing, who helped us get the word out about our new book.

Our children—Milaina, Noah (Elisia), Annalyse, and Micah—have provided many practical examples over the years of doing family devotions amid the milk spills, laughter, and questions. It's been a joy to watch you grow in your faith as you spread you wings and fly.

Our parents—Ron and the late Barbara Reaoch, and Ralph and Nancy Kyro—have always cheered us on, providing endless love and support. Ron was passionate about seeing this project come to fruition, and we're so thankful the Lord enabled it to happen.

We're grateful for our church family—Three Rivers Grace Church in Pittsburgh—who have been our family away from family for over two decades. Your support and enthusiasm for our project have meant so much.

Finally, we're thankful to our heavenly Father, who loves to give good gifts to His children (James 1:17). We pray the words in this book will guide our readers to know and love Him more as they discover His beautiful plan of redemption.

STACY AND BEN REAOCH

NOTES

1. A version of this lesson was written by Barbara Reaoch and previously published at Revive Our Hearts as part of the "Word in the Home" Easter blog series (2021), https://www.reviveourhearts.com/.
2. Ibid.
3. Ibid.
4. Ibid.
5. Ibid.
6. Ibid.
7. Ibid.
8. Ibid.
9. Ibid.
10. Ibid.